DT
731
.L772

Livingstone, David, 1813–1873.
  The Zambesi doctors; David Livingstone's letters to John
Kirk, 1858:1872, edited, with an introd. by R. Foskett.
Edinburgh, University Press [°1964]

  187 p. illus. (part col.) facsim., map, ports. 23 cm.

  1. Africa, Central—Descr. & trav.   i. Kirk, Sir John, 1832–1922
ii. Title.

DT731.L772   923.942 11/2/79   65–1280

THE ZAMBESI DOCTORS

THE ZAMBESI DOCTORS

Dr David Livingstone. This signed photograph was presented by
Livingstone to Mrs Webb of Newstead Abbey.

THE ZAMBESI DOCTORS
David Livingstone's Letters to John Kirk
1858:1872

edited, with an introduction by
R. FOSKETT

EDINBURGH
at the University Press

© R. FOSKETT 1964

EDINBURGH UNIVERSITY PRESS
One George Square, Edinburgh 8
United States and Canada
Aldine Publishing Co.
64 East Van Buren Street, Chicago 5
Australia and New Zealand
Hodder & Stoughton Ltd.
429 Kent Street, Sydney
425 Little Collins Street, Melbourne
41 Shortland Street, Auckland

Printed in Great Britain
By R. & R. Clark, Ltd., Edinburgh

CONTENTS

EDITORIAL NOTE

The Livingstone-Kirk correspondence is preserved among the family papers of three of Sir John Kirk's grandchildren, Mrs Daphne Foskett, Mrs Betty Verschoyle and Mr Geoffrey Bevington. It is contained, for the most part, in the *Kirk Papers* which belong to my wife, Daphne Foskett, but letters 25, 27, 32, 36, 42, 51, 54 and the second letter of the appendix are owned by Mrs Verschoyle and letters 58 and 60 by Mr Bevington. The Scottish National Memorial to David Livingstone at Blantyre now possess letter 5; letters 61, 62, 63 have recently been acquired by the National Library of Scotland and letter 64 is at Peace Museum, Zanzibar. I am most grateful for permission to publish all these letters. My thanks are also due to Mr Richard Gatty of Pepper Arden, Northallerton, for the use of an interesting letter from Agnes Livingstone to Mrs Webb, a signed photograph of David Livingstone and a photograph of Tom and Agnes Livingstone at Newstead Abbey, with Susi, Chuma, the Rev. H. Waller, and Mr and Mrs Webb – all from the Webb Papers. To Professor G. Shepperson and Dr A. Ross, of the University of Edinburgh, I also wish to express my thanks for their valuable help and advice.

Some of the letters have already been published by the late Professor Sir R. Coupland in his *Kirk on the Zambesi*[1] (numbers 1-11) and in his *Livingstone's Last Journey*[2] (numbers 61-63).

[1] Oxford, at the Clarendon Press, 1928.
[2] London, Collins, 1947.

Apart from adding punctuation in a few cases when it was thought that this would greatly help intelligibility, no attempt has been made to clarify Livingstone's meaning where the text is obscure. Livingstone's original spelling of place names has been retained in the text of the letters but modern forms have been used in the Introduction and in the Notes. The spelling of Zambesi is so closely associated with the Livingstone-Kirk story that it was felt that the retention of the original spelling would be more appropriate.

The fact that, during this period, Kirk and Livingstone were seldom apart for more than a few days at a time, explains why there is a gap in the correspondence between November 1859 and June 1863. They were busily engaged in exploring the Zambesi, Shire and Rovuma and in searching for the Great Lake about which they had heard from the natives and which together they eventually 'discovered'.

R. Foskett.

LIST OF ILLUSTRATIONS

INTRODUCTION

The series of letters written by Dr David Livingstone to Dr (later Sir) John Kirk, and now published in this volume, began in 1858 when the two men were first brought together over the preparations for the British Government Expedition to the Zambesi, which Livingstone had been invited to lead. The correspondence concluded in 1872, one year before the explorer's death at Chitambo's village, Ilala, at a time when he was completely cut off from the civilised world and Kirk was British Consul and Political Agent at Zanzibar.

The letters fall into four distinct groups but they are bound together by a connecting thread, a common interest in African exploration with a view to suppressing the slave trade which had its centre and market at Zanzibar. The first group of letters relates to the Zambesi Expedition and covers the period of preparation in England, the actual course of the exploration of the Zambesi and the journey which Livingstone made to Lake Nyasa, with the Makololo, before returning to England in 1864. The second group consists of letters written mainly from Newstead Abbey near Nottingham, the home of his friends Mr and Mrs W. F. Webb, with whom he stayed for several months before returning to Africa for what proved to be the last time. The third group of letters was written from India, when Livingstone was *en route* for Africa and had broken his journey at Bombay in order to dispose of the *Lady Nyassa* which he had left behind in 1864, on his way back to London. At this time Kirk was still in England and undecided as to his own future. The last group of letters is perhaps the most interesting, for it contains those written between 1867 and 1872 when no one in Britain knew where Livingstone could be found or whether he was dead or alive.

As the story of the great explorer's life has been told so frequently and in so much detail, it is unnecessary to repeat it here, except where it has a direct bearing upon the letters which he wrote to Kirk. In the case of his correspondent, the situation is entirely different for only a few of his papers have been published and no definitive biography has yet been written. His extensive journal of the Zambesi Expedition has never been made public in its entirety, although Sir Reginald Coupland made use of it in his book *Kirk on the Zambesi*.[1] Kirk is therefore little known except to specialists in African Studies and he has been almost completely over-shadowed by the leader whom he served so loyally on the Zambesi from 1858 to 1863 as Second in Command, Botanist, and Medical Officer of the Government Expedition. He did, however, play an important part not only in opening up the Dark Continent but also in putting an end to the slave trade on the east coast. It is desirable, in view of these facts, to give an outline of Kirk's career prior to his meeting with Livingstone as well as to say something about the part he played in African affairs during the period covered by the Livingstone-Kirk correspondence.

John Kirk was born in the Manse of Barry in Forfarshire on December 19, 1832, the second son of the Reverend John Kirk and his wife Christian Carnegie, and received his early education at the local High School at Arbroath. At the age of 15 he entered the University of Edinburgh and spent two years in the faculty of Arts before transferring in 1849 to the Medical School, graduating M.D. in 1854 and later in the

[1] R. Coupland, *Kirk on the Zambesi*, Oxford, 1928.

same year obtaining his L.R.C.S.(Edinburgh). He then received his first appointment, as Resident Physician at the Edinburgh Royal Infirmary, where he was a contemporary of Joseph Lister.

As a youth, Kirk had always shewn a keen interest in photography, an art which was then in its infancy, and it remained one of his hobbies until he was compelled to give it up at an advanced age owing to failing eyesight. The wax negatives of some of the photographs taken on the Zambesi Expedition in 1859 still survive and prints have been taken from them nearly a hundred years later, some of them being used to illustrate this book.

Kirk, like his father, was an enthusiastic botanist and student of natural history from an early age, and when he came up to the University in 1847, he continued to interest himself in these subjects. As a medical student, he attended Professor J. H. Balfour's lectures and was elected a Fellow of the Edinburgh Botanical Society, shortly before he became a graduate member of the University.

When an attempt was made to meet the shortage of medical men in the Crimea by recruiting a Civil Medical Service in 1855, Kirk was among the volunteers and was posted as Assistant Physician to the British Hospital at Erenkevi on the Dardanelles, where in his spare time he explored the surrounding district with his friends and made excursions to Mount Ida and Mount Olympus. At a later date, he presented his collection of plants from these parts to the University of Edinburgh together with the botanical specimens he brought back from Egypt in 1856, as he returned from the Crimea.

Shortly after arriving in London, Kirk got in touch with the Royal Botanic Gardens at Kew where he continued his studies with the encouragement and guidance of its Director, Sir William Hooker. He did not, however, neglect his other interests, and when the Chair of Natural History became vacant at Queen's College at Kingston his former teacher, Professor Balfour, advised him to apply for the post. About the same time, it became known that a qualified botanist would shortly be required for the Expedition which the Government was proposing to send to the Zambesi in 1858 and when consulted about possible candidates for the post, both Balfour and Hooker recommended that it should be offered to Kirk. Before he had had time to apply for the Professorship at Kingston, Kirk was sounded informally about joining the Zambesi party and at once agreed to accept the offer, if it should be made to him. Livingstone, as soon as he received this news, sent him instructions about obtaining medical supplies and assumed that the Foreign Office would confirm the appointment. He gave Kirk authority to spend up to £15, and when he protested that the amount was totally inadequate for the purpose, admitted that a mistake had been made and amended the figure to £50!

By February 1858 all necessary preparations had been completed and Kirk was told to come up to Liverpool before the end of the month to embark for the voyage to the mouth of the Zambesi with the other members of the party. The Expedition left Birkenhead on March 10 on board s.s. *Pearl* and arrived at the Cape by the middle of April. A few days before they landed at Simon's Town, Kirk received his instructions as a member of the Expedition. Livingstone had prepared this lengthy document during the course of the voyage and dated it March 18, but he did not hand it over to Kirk until April 15. At the same time he gave him the written instructions from Professor Owen and Dr Joseph Hooker concerning his duties as Botanist and Zoologist.

During the exploration of the Zambesi and its tributaries Livingstone and Kirk were together for most of the time, but occasionally they separated to fulfil special assignments and kept in touch with one another by correspondence. From June until August, Kirk was left behind on Expedition Island and spent his time in botanical research and securing supplies of fresh meat for the party, while Livingstone went up the Zambesi as far as Sena. He was beginning to grow impatient and told Livingstone that he was anxious to go with him on his next trip up the river. By the end of July Livingstone was back at Expedition Island and when he set off again on August 2 Kirk joined him and helped to navigate the launch, as Commander Bedingfeld had resigned from the Expedition with the intention of returning to England. On this occasion the party went as far as Shupanga, returning to Expedition Island on August 5 and making the journey in less than a day. A few days later, Livingstone, Baines and Kirk again went up to Shupanga, making their headquarters with Colonel Nuñez, the Portuguese Commandant. Kirk remained there for some weeks while other members of the party took stores further up the river. When Livingstone reached the Island of Pita, above Sena, he wrote to Kirk on August 25 telling him of the difficulty they had had in navigating the river and asking for his support in the case of Bedingfeld. From the letter it is obvious that Livingstone was not entirely satisfied with the way in which he had handled the dispute with Bedingfeld.[1] He told Kirk that a report would have to be sent on the whole affair to the Foreign Office and that he would like to have his testimony as to the filthy condition of the *Ma Robert*. He had no wish to give the impression of having acted harshly in the matter and desired Kirk to support him by saying that Bedingfeld's resignation had been necessary in the interest of the Expedition, adding that his testimony would carry weight with the Foreign Office.

[1] A full account of the dispute is given in J. R. P. Wallis, *Life of Thomas Baines*, Cape, 1941.

When some months later Livingstone dismissed Richard Thornton and Thomas Baines from the Expedition, he again wrote to Kirk asking for his assistance. In a letter dated October 17, 1859, he instructed him to proceed overland to Tete with Rae, the ship's engineer, and escort the two men down to the coast and see them safely embarked for England on a man-of-war which was expected to call for them at Kongone Harbour. Kirk was also required to search Baines' personal baggage for any property belonging to the British Government and to take possession of the storekeeper's book. It was an unpleasant task for anyone to be asked to perform but Kirk managed to do it with great tact. For his part, he disbelieved the charges of dishonesty which Livingstone had made and always took the view that Baines was innocent.

On October 29, 1859, Livingstone sent a note to Kirk saying he intended to go down to Shupanga from Shamoara and would wait for him there, but shortly after the letter had been sent, he found he was unable to keep the appointment as the *Ma Robert* had begun to sink. Instead he stayed on at Shamoara and wrote on November 6 to say he had decided to go down to the coast, although it would mean keeping the pumps working almost continuously, as the boat was making a good deal of water, but that the whaler would be left behind for Kirk's own use.

No further letters passed between the two men until 1863, a few weeks before Kirk left the Expedition and made his way back to England. By this date, Livingstone had been informed of the Expedition's recall, but he had made up his mind, before returning home, to undertake another journey to Lake Nyasa. On June 2 he was at Murchison Cataracts and sent Kirk a letter, asking him to settle certain accounts on his behalf and giving him news about two members of the Universities Mission to Central Africa, Lovell Proctor

Dr John Kirk

and Horace Waller, and about James Stewart of the Scottish Free Kirk, who had come up from the Cape with Mrs Livingstone some years before and who did not appear to recognise cotton bushes when he saw them! At the conclusion of this letter, Livingstone wrote 'I am sure I wish you every success in your future life. You were always a right hand to me and I never trusted you in vain.'[1]

About a month later, in a letter dated July 5, Livingstone again wrote to Kirk from the Cataracts, telling of his plans for the future. He intended to dismantle the *Lady Nyassa* and sell her in India, but before doing so, he wanted to make a trip to the north end of Lake Nyasa with the Makololo. The letter also contained news about the Universities Mission and first impressions of the Right Reverend W. G. Tozer who had been appointed in 1863 to succeed Bishop C. F. Mackenzie and whom he described as 'a good cautious man'.

Kirk was now on his way to England and wrote a number of letters which reached Livingstone by the beginning of August and informed him of his movements since leaving the Zambesi. Setting out on July 4, he got as far as Mozambique and was then held up for some weeks, waiting for a ship to take him on to Zanzibar. He received another letter from Livingstone, dated August 8, giving more news of the Universities Mission and hinting that Bishop Tozer intended to withdraw from the mainland and set up his headquarters in Madagascar. Livingstone strongly disagreed with this policy, which he took to mean a permanent abandonment of the African continent. But in this he was mistaken, for Tozer did not move to Madagascar; instead he established himself at Zanzibar, with a view to an ultimate return to the Zambesi area. The same letter referred to a leakage of the contents of a Government dispatch relating to the work

[1] Letter 18, page 64.

of the Expedition. Livingstone thought that the Governor at the Cape had shown this dispatch to Dr Steere before forwarding it to him. The dispatch contained a complaint that the Government had received only scanty information about the resources of the country; this was, in Livingstone's opinion, quite unfair and he intended to ask Sir William Hooker to say whether the materials which Kirk had sent to Kew were or were not ample for the illustration of the material productions of a wild and undeveloped country.

Kirk reached Southampton on October 9. Livingstone was still in Africa, and, in a letter written from the Murchison Cataracts dated December 9, gave Kirk a description of the journey to the sources of the Loangwa and the latest news about the Universities Mission. Horace Waller had decided to return to England and it was rumoured that the Bishop now intended to transfer the Mission from the Zambesi to Madagascar, as the unhealthy climate of Morambala made it impossible for its members to remain there any longer. The letter also contained a reference to a rumour that Livingstone had been murdered up at the Lake, together with the Governor of Tete's wife and daughter!

Early in 1864 Livingstone was ready to return home, and, leaving the Zambesi in January, he made his way down the coast to Quilimane with the *Pioneer* and the *Lady Nyassa*, reaching the mouth of the Kongone by February 13. Two British cruisers were anchored in the harbour, and when Livingstone discovered they were bound for Mozambique, he persuaded them to take the two vessels in tow. When they arrived at Mozambique he handed over the *Pioneer* for dispatch to the Cape. He retained the *Lady Nyassa* and on April 16 set out for Zanzibar with the intention of selling her there, leaving Waller and the rest of the Mission party to make the voyage to the Cape in the *Pioneer*. It was unfortunate for Livingstone that Rae, who had accompanied him as far as Zanzibar, now determined to leave and go on to Johanna, for it placed him in a dilemma. As it had proved impossible to effect a suitable sale of the *Lady Nyassa*, Livingstone wanted to take her across the Indian Ocean to Bombay. At such short notice, he could not expect to obtain a suitable successor to Rae as ship's engineer, and he decided to make the voyage without one and to risk the danger of running into the monsoon. In forty-five days the vessel crossed 2,500 miles of ocean and arrived in Bombay just one day before the monsoon was due to break, a remarkable feat, which, however, attracted no attention at the time and Livingstone wrote in his journal 'the vessel was so small that no one noticed our arrival'. After spending less than a month in India Livingstone embarked for England, leaving Bombay on June 24 and reaching London on July 23. The same day he called upon Sir Roderick and Lady Murchison and had an interview with Lord Palmerston before writing to Kirk from the Tavistock Hotel, Covent Garden, on July 28. By this date he had already made up his mind to return to Africa to continue his exploration of the interior. This may have been one reason for not selling the *Lady Nyassa* in Bombay (which had been his original intention), and why instead he left it with Captain Young for safe keeping, while he came home for consultations with the Government. The task of suppressing the African slave trade was never far from his thoughts: he had seen far too much of its ramifications in the course of his travels ever to forget its horror or the widespread misery which inevitably followed in its train.

After some very full weeks in the south of England, when he was busily occupied with public engagements and private interviews, Livingstone travelled up to Scotland and, from his home in Hamilton, toured the west coast, visiting Staffa, Iona, Ulva and Mull. He much enjoyed this Scottish excursion, but when he wrote to Kirk on September 1 from Hamilton, he was a little anxious about his health and intended to consult Professor Syme within the next few weeks.

Long before he arrived in England Livingstone's proposal to come home was known to his friends, and, while still in Bombay, he received an invitation from Mr and Mrs W. F. Webb to visit them at their mansion in Nottinghamshire, Newstead Abbey, and remain with them as long as he could. The invitation was renewed when he reached London, and after a little persuasion he agreed to accept it, although he had no intention of remaining with the Webbs for any great length of time. In fact, he did not leave Newstead until April 1865, and he wrote up his journals of the Zambesi Expedition into his book *The Zambesi and its Tributaries* during the months he spent as their guest.

Livingstone's friendship with William Frederick Webb began as a result of an accidental meeting which took place when Livingstone was returning with his family from Lake N'gami and Webb was big game hunting around Colesberg. Born in 1829 and educated at Eton, Webb intended to make the army his career and obtained a Commission in the 17th Lancers, but he soon found that a soldier's life in peace-time was apt to be very monotonous and resigned his Commission in favour of his brother. In December 1850 he went out to the Cape and travelled widely in a country swarming with game and almost unexplored, making Colesberg his headquarters. On one occasion, he was seriously ill with fever and might have died but for the fact that Livingstone sought him out and gave him medical attention. He had heard through natives that an unknown white man was very ill somewhere in the neighbourhood and at once set off on foot to find the stranger, taking with him such remedies as experience led him to suppose might be of use. That was the first time the two men met, and later in life Webb always

claimed that he owed his life to Livingstone's timely assistance and that it marked the beginning of their life-long
friendship.

After such a long absence from Britain, Livingstone was
anxious to be reunited with his family and this made him
reluctant to accept the Webbs' offer of hospitality, but one
by one the objections he raised were overcome. Mrs Webb
told him to bring his daughter Agnes to stay with him at
Newstead, promising to arrange for her to have music les-
sons while she was there and offering to have the two boys
as her guests for part of the Christmas holidays. In the face
of such generosity, there was no more to be said, and
Livingstone came to stay with the Webbs in September
1864, bringing Agnes with him and entering upon what Sir
H. H. Johnston once described as 'perhaps all things considered, the eight happiest months of his life'.

Until its dissolution, the Priory of Newstead, which had
been founded in 1170 or thereabouts by King Henry II in
expiation of the murder of Thomas à Becket, was one of the
most flourishing monastic houses in the Midlands. The
great priory church still remains as a splendid ruin, its sad
condition being due as much to the damage received during
the Civil War as to the violence of the Reformation. The
adjacent mansion had been bought by Webb at the time of
his marriage, as none of the houses he had inherited with
his estates were considered suitable residences for his bride.
A former owner of the property, Colonel Wildman, who
had been for many years an equerry to the Duke of Sussex,
added the tower which he named after him, the Sussex
Tower, and this was the part of the mansion occupied by
Livingstone during his residence at Newstead.

Webb's daughter, Alice, gives an interesting account of
the explorer at this time. In her book, *Livingstone and Newstead*, she wrote, 'he was always extremely neat and careful

in his appearance although even apart from his predilection for his gold banded cap, there was nothing in the least clerical about his dress'.[1] Mrs Webb normally read the daily prayers for the family, but when Livingstone was present, he always performed this duty for her and on Sundays went along with the rest of the household to the private chapel, for Morning and Evening Prayer which were read by the chaplain, the Reverend Curtis Jackson; in these and in many other ways he identified himself with the activities of his hosts. During these months, Agnes Livingstone was prepared for confirmation and received the rite at the hands of the Bishop of Lincoln, making her first communion in the chapel at Newstead. Her father communicated on this occasion and took the Sacrament with her regularly each month while he remained with the Webbs.

Much of Livingstone's day was passed compiling his book about the Zambesi and its tributaries,[2] and he usually devoted the morning to this task which he found somewhat laborious, especially when it came to the production of the fair copy for the use of the publisher. A number of friends helped him, among them W. C. Oswell, the hunter and explorer, who read and corrected the manuscript before it was sent off to John Murray, the publisher. Other friends helped to improve the literary style and Kirk provided information about animals and plants as well as native words. By April 15 the whole work was ready, and ten days later Livingstone and his daughter went up to the Metropolis.

In December 1864 Mr Haywood, Q.C., came to spend a few days at Newstead and on behalf of Lord Palmerston asked Livingstone what he desired the Government to do for him and his family. With no thought for himself or of

[1] A. Z. Frazer, *Livingstone and Newstead*, Murray, 1913, page 89.
[2] D. and C. Livingstone, *Narrative of an Expedition to the Zambesi and its Tributaries*, etc. Murray, 1865.

securing any material advantage, he merely asked for free access to the African Highlands by the Zambesi and Shire rivers to be formally ratified by treaty with Portugal. It never occurred to him to ask for a pension or a salary for his services to the country, and when he was given an official Commission over the African chiefs from the Portuguese boundary to Abyssinia, he was told he could expect neither a salary nor a pension. Many years later, when he was lost and alone in the heart of Africa, he recalled this meeting with Mr Haywood at Newstead and bitterly regretted that he had made no material demands of the British Government.

While he was working at his book about the Zambesi and its tributaries, Livingstone was in constant correspondence with Kirk. He had purposely avoided dealing with the botany and natural history of the Zambesi as he hoped Kirk would publish a separate work on these subjects and wrote to him on October 21, 1864, saying he would offer him every assistance, if he would do something about it. He was also concerned to know about Kirk's plans for the future, and in a letter dated November 7, asked what he intended to do and offered to testify to his abilities. A week later, he extended on behalf of the Webbs an invitation to Kirk to visit Newstead, and mentioned that his brother Charles was bringing his American wife to join them for a short time. Receiving no reply, he wrote to Kirk again on November 24, renewing the invitation, urging him to accept and also to agree to speak at a meeting which Mr Webb had arranged in the Mechanics' Institute at Mansfield. Livingstone wanted his former Second in Command to meet some of the influential people who were visiting the Webbs and to obtain for him an appointment in the Colonial or Foreign Office. Other letters followed in swift succession containing requests of many different kinds. Would Kirk see Colonel Rigby at the Colonial Office and would he be willing to lend some of his photographs to his publisher's artist? Would he make an effort to come up to Newstead? And when Kirk agreed to stay with the Webbs immediately after Christmas, Livingstone asked him to cash a cheque and purchase a black doll for one of the children at Newstead.

On February 13, 1865, Kirk heard that a box had been found at the Cape which contained specimens in bottles and had been brought back to England by the Reverend C. A. Alington. It had been supposed that the box belonged to Thornton, but Livingstone thought otherwise and believing it to contain Kirk's lost specimens, directed it to be forwarded with a covering note to Dr Hooker at Kew. During March Livingstone frequently wrote to ask Kirk for information about particular African plants and to enquire what steps he had taken to secure a suitable Government post; he was anxious to see his former colleague placed, if possible, somewhere on the east coast of Africa.

On May 13, 1865, Livingstone took the opportunity of calling on his publisher to discuss the illustrations for his forthcoming book, before he set off once more for Africa. Plans for his next expedition were already being formulated and he told Kirk he would be delighted to have him as a companion, but that the funds available would not run to a salary. Alington had asked to accompany him at his own expense, but Livingstone was not keen on having another untried European on his African travels, because of his previous unfortunate experiences on the Zambesi Expedition with Baines and Thornton. He admitted, however, that Alington was a 'good fellow' with some knowledge of Zulu.

Kirk was still doing research at Kew in a voluntary capacity and had not yet decided what was to be his next step.

Meanwhile, Livingstone came up to Scotland, having completed his engagements in London, and arrived at Hamilton towards the end of May, only to find that his mother had become seriously ill and was so confused in mind that she was unable to recognise him and took him to be one of his own sons. He realised that the end was not far distant, but when she rallied a little, he decided to hurry down to Oxford to fulfil a speaking engagement. Shortly after his arrival he received the sad news of his mother's death and immediately returned to Hamilton in time for the funeral. Kirk had suffered a similar bereavement about this time and Livingstone sent him a short note on June 24 expressing his sympathy, 'the more cordial inasmuch as we have had the same tender ties severed'.[1]

Shortly after this, Livingstone returned to Newstead and wrote to Kirk on July 30 about Thomas Baines. Baines had been demanding that Livingstone should admit publicly that he had treated him unjustly by dismissing him from the Zambesi Expedition. Livingstone refused to make any such admission and insisted that he had been perfectly justified in the action he had taken.[2] Early in August he said goodbye to Newstead and travelled up to London, where he visited the Zoological Gardens with Kirk and the Webbs on August 8. The next day his friends returned to Nottingham and Livingstone wrote in his journal 'parted from my friends, Mr and Mrs Webb at Kings Cross Station today. He gracefully said he wished I had been coming rather than going away and she shook me very cordially by both hands and said "you will come back to us again, wont you?"'[3]

The next few days were spent in paying a few final visits prior to his departure from London. On August 11 he took

---

1 Letter 51, page 119.
2 See Letter 52.
3 Quoted by A. Z. Frazer in *Livingstone and Newstead*, page 163.

leave of the Foreign Office and attended a dinner with his publisher, John Murray, on the same day. One of his last acts was to place Agnes in the care of his old friend W. C. Oswell before setting sail for Bombay on the first stage of his voyage to the east coast of Africa.

Arriving in Bombay on September 11, Livingstone at once went to call upon the Governor, Sir Bartle Frere, and enlisted his help in recruiting a party of natives to accompany him to Africa. Before leaving for Zanzibar, he had to dispose of the *Lady Nyassa* in order to augment his slender resources. In the end he was forced to sell the vessel, which cost £6,000, for the modest sum of £2,300. About this time, news reached Bombay that Colonel Playfair, the British Consul at Zanzibar had been taken ill and had returned to England; although no resignation had yet taken place, it was thought unlikely that he would be able to resume his duties and that he would shortly be replaced. Here was just the kind of post Livingstone wished to secure for his former colleague, and he wrote from Poona, on September 20, urging Kirk to ask Lord Dalhousie to consider him for the post, in the event of Playfair's resignation. Receiving no immediate reply, Livingstone sent another letter written on November 17 from Bombay, enquiring how matters stood. Meantime another suitable vacancy was impending owing to the resignation of Dr Birdwood, the Curator of the Bombay Botanical Garden and Museum, and Livingstone informed Kirk that he was being recommended for this post. There was still no reply from Kirk, and Livingstone, having completed his preparations, was about to embark on the *Thule* without knowing if his efforts on Kirk's behalf had been successful, when Sir Bartle Frere enquired about his suitability for an appointment at Zanzibar. As the *Thule* did not sail until the New Year, Livingstone had time to advise Kirk of the enquiries which were being made about him and of his probable appointment to some Government post, but no definite appointment had been made when he left India on January 2, 1866. He had hoped to obtain for Kirk the consulate vacated by Playfair, but the Bombay Government had other ideas and promoted Dr G. E. Seward, the Agency Surgeon, to the rank of Consul, offering Kirk the lesser post of Agency Surgeon. Although he was about to be married (and Zanzibar was not a very suitable place for a young bride), Kirk decided to accept the offer, and his fiancée, Helen Cook, came out to marry him, shortly after his arrival at Zanzibar.

On March 19, 1866, Livingstone and his party of 13 Indian sepoys, 9 Nassick boys, 10 Johanna men, 2 Shupanga men, 2 Yaos – Chuma and Wikatani, who were still in their 'teens – and 24 local Negroes, set out from Zanzibar for the interior. The plan was to go by sea to Mikindani, disembark and follow the course of the Rovuma to its source, cross Lake Nyasa to Kotakota and then march in a northerly direction as far as Ujiji on Lake Tanganyika. Ujiji was a suitable base for further exploration of the interior and was also on a trade route down to the coast which passed through Unyanyembe. Livingstone did not follow this direct route from the coast for he wanted to see more of Lake Nyasa; but he arranged for the Zanzibar firm of Ludha Damji to send a considerable supply of stores to him at Ujiji by this shorter way, and to deliver them to the firm's agent Thani ben Suellim.

As he penetrated further into the interior, Livingstone and his party became increasingly cut off from the outside world. The trade route was blocked from time to time by Arab slavers, and trustworthy carriers were hard to find, with the result that letters sent from the coast did not reach him, and many of his own letters failed to get through to their destination. The only white man to see him after he left Zanzibar in 1866 until his remains were brought back from Ujiji in 1874 was H. M. Stanley, the American journalist, who had been sent by his newspaper, the *New York Herald*, to 'find Livingstone'. Accidentally stumbling across Livingstone's tracks, Stanley followed him to Ujiji in 1871, coming face to face with him on November 10 and greeting him with the formal phrase 'Dr Livingstone, I presume'.

During these years news came through to England at rare intervals that the explorer was still alive and well; but his family had long periods of anxious waiting for letters to tell them of his doings. Agnes was relieved to learn that in October 1867 her father had arrived safely at Ujiji, for a rumour had been widely circulated in Zanzibar, with much circumstantial evidence to support it, that he had been murdered by the Mazitu in the region of Lake Nyasa. The story had come from Musa Kamaals[1] and the Johanna men who had been with him on a journey into the interior. Livingstone had reached Marenga's in September 1866 when he was deserted by the Johanna men, who made their way back to the coast, arriving in Zanzibar on December 6. To cover up their dismal conduct, these men had concocted the story of Livingstone's murder and told it at the British Consulate, where in the face of careful cross-examination, they adhered to every detail of their story. Kirk reluctantly came to the conclusion that they were speaking the truth. When the news of his supposed death reached England, it was generally accepted, although a few of Livingstone's friends, among them Lieutenant E. D. Young, who had had dealings with Musa, refused to believe it. Young offered to lead an expedition to Lake Nyasa to prove its falsity, an

---

[1] One of the Johanna men whom Livingstone engaged at Zanzibar to accompany him into the interior. He deserted and spread a rumour that Livingstone had been murdered near Lake Nyasa, repeating his story to Kirk on his return to the coast in December 1866.

offer which was quickly taken up by the Royal Geographical Society, and in 1867 a party set out for Africa and Lake Nyasa. Although unable to locate the lost explorer, the expedition was successful in establishing the probability that he was still alive, and this was turned into certainty when a Swahili slave told them he had seen a white man, quite alone, to the north of Lake Nyasa and engaged in no trade. Further news was received in November of a white man travelling alone in the interior, and in January 1868 Seward's successor as British Consul at Zanzibar, H. A. Churchill, received a packet of letters from Livingstone.

It took many months for letters to reach England, and Livingstone had no idea of the anxiety which he was causing among his family and friends. News did not reach him of the Young Expedition until 1870, and he was quite out of touch with what was happening in the outside world, a fact which is evident from the last few letters he wrote to Kirk and Playfair.

During the early autumn of 1868 Livingstone was near to Mpweto's and hoped to join Mohamed bin Saleh on a trip to Manyema, to the west of Lake Tanganyika; but the plan fell through, and instead he made for his base at Ujiji, arriving there, after many delays, on March 14, 1869. He was now in a very weak condition and greatly in need of rest, good food and medicine. Ample stores and a stock of cloth and beads had been sent up to Ujiji from the coast and ought to have been awaiting him; instead he found the wine and cheese had been left with the medicines at Unyanyembe, some distance away, and the best of the cloth and beads had been stolen.

While at Ujiji, Livingstone wrote at least forty-two letters, but none of them reached their destination with the exception of one dated May 30, to Kirk and Playfair, which had got through to the coast. In it he complained of Musa

Kamaals's dishonesty and of the difficulty of finding carriers who could be trusted to deliver safely the letters handed to them. He also mentioned some of the plans he had made for the future, with the source of the Nile very much in his mind.

Instead of waiting at Ujiji for the 'new squad' as he called the porters who were being sent up from the coast, he decided to set out for Manyema and to pick them up on his return to his base, as the journey was not expected to take more than four or five months. At the outset all went smoothly, and Bambarre, a fairly important place in Manyema some 100 miles to the west of Tanganyika, was reached by September 21, 1869. On arriving there, Livingstone found that the whole district had recently been disturbed by Arab slavers with the unfortunate result of creating a hostile native population; this made it impossible to continue his travels in Manyema. There was no alternative but to return to Bambarre, and he arrived there on December 19, moving off again seven days later in an attempt to reach Lualaba. Progress, however, was very slow in view of the heavy rains; to add to his troubles he had ulcers on both feet, and the porters had deserted. Within seven months, he was back at Bambarre where he remained for the next eight months, immobilised and frustrated by his misfortune. When he wrote to Kirk and Playfair on November 2, 1870, Livingstone was still waiting for letters; the only news he had received since 1866 was contained in a few copies of the *Saturday Review* and *Punch* which had got through to him. He was running short of paper and for this reason was unable to write separate letters to Kirk and Playfair, as otherwise he would have done.

The long expected reinforcements from Zanzibar, when they arrived, proved quite useless; for not only did they behave in a truculent manner from the moment they arrived in Bambarre, they also spread it around that Consul Kirk

had really sent them to bring Livingstone back with them
to the coast and firmly refused to go with him further into
the interior. They were at length persuaded to change their
minds, with the help of Mohamad Bogharib who threat-
ened them with his pistol, and the party set off from Bambarre, reaching Nyangwe on March 29, 1871, and for the
first time Livingstone was able to see the River Lualaba.

A few letters, written many months before, were delivered
to Livingstone at this time, including one from Kirk dated
February 28, 1869, which enclosed another from his daughter Agnes. He replied, almost by return, from Webb's
Lualaba or Lacustrine River on March 25, 1871, recalling
how Lord Palmerston had once enquired what he could do
to help him, when he was staying at Newstead Abbey, and
how at the time he had been quite unaware of what this
meant. He also expressed concern that arm-chair critics at
home might accuse him of overdrawing the picture, if he
made public some of the episodes he had witnessed in the
heart of Africa.

Livingstone was unable to leave Nyangwe until canoes
were available and the slaves of the Banian tried to mutiny
in an effort to make him return to Zanzibar instead of pressing further into the interior, as he wished to do. The situation became even more serious when one of the Arab traders
at Nyangwe, Abed, discovered a plot to kill him, and it
became impossible for him to trust the Banians any more.
On May 14 he wrote to Kirk about his difficulty in obtaining a canoe and the insubordinate conduct of the slaves who
had demanded an extortionate increase in wages. He was
now without writing-paper, except for a piece of blue wrap-
ing paper on which had been written the word 'quinine' and
the initials 'J. K.' (John Kirk); and for ink he had to use a
red native dye. The weeks passed slowly by with Livingstone, still at Nyangwe and unable to get the canoe he

wanted, and on June 14 he noted in his journal 'Hassani got nine canoes and put sixty-three persons in three; I cannot get one'. Two days later he wrote to Kirk on the reverse side of the blue wrapper, referring to the bountiful provisions which had been sent to him with immense difficulty from the coast and which had been misused by Sherif the Arab trader, thus reducing him to beggary. With the help of Dugumbe, the wealthiest and most influential of the Arab traders, he intended to buy a canoe and go up the River Lualaba to Kamolondo, but the existence of another cataract compelled him to alter his plans.

Livingstone was still in a very weak condition and his mind was confused, but it made no difference to his resolve to go on rather than retrace his steps to the coast. He wanted to get as far as Katanga and see for himself what he believed to be the sources of the Nile; but Dugumbe was either unable, or more probably unwilling, to come to his assistance and a massacre[1] in the market-place at Nyangwe on July 15 made the achievement of this objective quite impossible. There was no alternative but to return to Ujiji with his unsatisfactory Banian slaves. Setting out for his base on July 20, Livingstone and his party did not arrive at Ujiji until October only to discover that the medical supplies and other stores had been sold by Sherif and that he was not only without the bare necessities of life but also without the means of obtaining them. His position was one of extreme difficulty and he was almost at his wits' end when suddenly and unexpectedly help reached him from the outside world. On October 28, 1871, Susi[2] came running up to him at top speed and gasped out 'an Englishman, I see

---

[1] Letter 61, page 145.
[2] One of the two Africans who were with Livingstone when he died and who brought his body to the coast. He was first employed at Shupanga to help construct the *Lady Nyassa*.

Arab Sheiks at Lamu. Photograph by Kirk.

him' and then hastened away to meet H. M. Stanley and his well-equipped caravan, which brought medicines and other much needed supplies. The American journalist had 'found Livingstone'.

The two men remained together until March 14, 1872, when Stanley left for Zanzibar, taking with him three important documents and the Doctor's precious journal, which had been fastened with five seals. During the months they spent together, Stanley was able to persuade Livingstone that the British Consul on the east coast was to blame for many of his difficulties and Kirk was much hurt when he received a letter dated October 30, 1871, which ended with these words: 'I feel inclined to relinquish the hope of ever getting help from Zanzibar to finish the little work I have to do. . . . I may wait twenty years and your slaves feast and fail.' A chance visit from Livingstone's son Oswell enabled Kirk to clear up the misunderstanding, for when he heard about his father's letter, he at once wrote to him, with the pleasing result that a further communication was received in which Livingstone wrote:

My dear Kirk,
I am sorry to hear by a note from Oswell that you had taken my formal complaint against certain Banyans and Arabs as a covert attack upon yourself; this grieves me deeply, for it is a result I never intended to produce.

The story of Stanley's public attack on Kirk's conduct at Zanzibar and of Livingstone's last travels and lonely death fall outside the scope of this work; but it is interesting to note that in Kirk's copy of *Livingstone's Last Journals*, Vol. 11,[1] Kirk wrote in pencil at the top of page 129 '26th June, friendly letter from Livingstone. This shews he had

---

[1] This volume is now in the possession of Kirk's granddaughter, Mrs Daphne Foskett.

Z.D.— C

received the Quinine from me'. The existence of the blue wrapper marked 'quinine' and 'J. K.' which was used as writing-paper for two letters to Kirk in 1871 confirms this statement.

The letters published in this volume reveal that Kirk was regarded by the great explorer not only as a competent botanist and physician whom, but for lack of finance, he would have taken with him on what turned out to be his last African journey, but also as a congenial companion who shared his determination to bring to an end the slave trade on the east coast of Africa.

Livingstone died at Chitambo's village, Ilala, on May 1, 1873, without completing his life-long ambition to destroy the trade at its source.

Kirk continued to exercise a considerable influence, not only in Zanzibar but on the whole of the east coast, as British Consul General from 1873 until his enforced retirement in 1887. On returning to England, he made his home at Sevenoaks in Kent and continued to take an active interest in Central African affairs for the rest of his life. He was appointed British Plenipotentiary at the Brussels International Conference in 1889 and Special Commissioner to the Niger in 1895. His advice was frequently sought by the younger generation of African administrators, amongst whom was Lugard, and no better summary of Kirk's career and influence can be given than that written by Lugard in September 1921, just two years before Kirk's death:

Sir John Kirk is the last of that great band of British explorers who laid open the secrets of the Dark Continent to Western civilisation. But he was much more than an explorer. As Consul General at Zanzibar he proved himself one of our astutest diplomats, as Germany had to admit. He won the entire confidence of the Sultan, Seyyid

Bargash, and induced him to sign the Edicts of 1875 and 1876, which should have put an end to slavery in his dominions in a short time. It was through his influence that Great Britain acquired East Africa and the Imperial British East Africa Company received a charter to develop it. He was British Plenipotentiary at the Brussels Conference and bore a large part in the drafting of the Act of 1892 which first embodied in an international treaty the moral obligations of the civilised nations towards the African races.

These were well known public services but for a quarter of a century after his retirement, he was ceaselessly engaged in work for Africa of which the world knew little. It was to him that all those interested in Central African questions – especially regarding the slave trade – turned for advice and he never failed to suggest a practical solution. As Vice-Chairman of the Uganda Railways Committee, as Foreign Secretary of the Royal Geographical Society, as Special Commissioner to the West Coast and in a score of other ways, he added to the services he rendered to Africa and to science. But he still found time to know personally and to assist with his advice and kind sympathy almost everyone who twenty or thirty years ago went to Africa. From my earliest African days in 1888, he has been my counsellor and friend, for whom admiration vies with affection and whose example it has been my greatest ambition to follow – the ablest, the most sympathetic, and the most modest of men.

Writing in the same year, Sir Harry Johnston, another distinguished African administrator, who knew Kirk well, paid this tribute:

I have always thought Sir John Kirk one of the greatest men produced by Great Britain during the 19th century.

The magnitude of his African researches – more especially in botany – was never properly appreciated until long after his official career was closed.

It still remains true that Kirk's great achievements have never been fully recognised and that he has been overshadowed by his contemporaries David Livingstone and Sir Bartle Frere.

ZAMBESI EXPEDITION
1858:1864

I

Hamilton
January 4th, 1858

My Dear Sir,

It was a matter of regret with me that in consequence of other matters pressing on my attention when you kindly called at Athol Place,[1] I neglected to ask your company to dinner in order to have more conversation together. I saw you in the distance and the servant gave chase but she said that you suddenly vanished and your note of the 1st January explained why.

I was absent the whole of Saturday and now before starting for London (20 Bedford Square) answer your questions so far as I can.

The passages out and home will be defrayed by Government, the contemplated length of the Expedition is two years but there is a possibility of its being prolonged beyond that period by circumstances of which we are not at present aware.

With regard to the 'necessary expenses' I am not quite clear as to what you mean; suppose you shoot a buffalo, there will be no expense incurred in cooking and eating it. There are no inns or hotels in the country. The lodging will be all free. The expedition will have supplies of plain food – coffee, sugar etc., and everything else I suppose will be got in the usual mess fashion, each member contributing a share of the expense of the extras. I shall not be answerable for luxuries of any kind whatever. An expedition of this kind cannot be successful unless all the members are willing to 'rough it' and it will be well if we all thoroughly understand this before setting out. The salary is £350 per annum.

If you are prepared to rough it when necessary, I shall feel obliged by a note to that effect and will then recommend your name to Lord Clarendon.[2]

I may mention that as a knowledge of the plants and woods already used in dyeing or suitable for dyestuffs – medicines, fibrous substances and gums – is expected from the Botanist of the Expedition, if you are still desirous of serving, additional familiarity with economic botany would be desirable.

A Mr Napier of Glasgow, known I believe to Dr Wilson,[3] has had his attention turned to dye stuffs and would be happy to give valuable hints if you thought them necessary.

I am etc
D. Livingstone

2

12 Kensington Palace Gardens
January 14th, 1858

My Dear Sir,

As it is desirable to have preparations in as forward a state as possible, I shall feel obliged if you make out a list of the medicines which you may deem necessary for the Expedition, bearing in mind that about £15 will be expended therein and that Fever will be the most common complaint.

The names given in to the Earl of Clarendon were mentioned at the Royal Society and also at the Royal Geographical Society. Dr Sharpey[4] at the former spoke in the kindest manner of your qualifications and it was thought that some questions relating to the Tsetse might possibly engage your attention, in addition to your botanical and medical duties. The final decision has not yet come from the Foreign Office but I have no doubt but it will be favourable in as far as you are concerned, and I shall lose no time in letting you know about it.

I am Dear Sir
Yours faithfully
David Livingstone

Dr Sharpey mentioned that your father was an old friend of his. If you are at home please to present my kindest regards to him. I hope you are getting yourself up in dye stuffs, gums etc, etc.

3

12 Kensington Palace Gardens
January 21st, 1858

My Dear Sir,

I found out yesterday that I had made a mistake in saying
£15 instead of £50 were allotted for the medicines and your
letter of this morning shews that you felt that the former
sum was rather stinted. I return the list and you will be
good enough to increase the quantities and also to order
them from some man in whom you have confidence. See
that they are ready and sent to Liverpool by the 1st February and let the account come to me before that time –
allow me to suggest a good stock of the Resin of Jalap. I
found a pill composed of that with calomel & quinine an
excellent remedy in fever – also Fowler's solution of arsenic
– a larger quantity of soda as it is very useful in allaying
obstinate vomiting – & a decided increase in Epsom salts for
the natives. The Quinine is not a whit too large. Increase
that too. It will be advisable to give quinine wine to all the
Europeans before entering and while in the Delta.

You will not I hope think me inclined to quackery if I
mention Warburg's drops as so highly spoken of in India
that I really think them worth a trial. If you agree in this a
little may be added but they are very dear. Enquire about
them and if you think they merit a trial we may have some.

Dont stint yourself in any thing that you feel assured will
aid your researches in dyestuffs and get the best of everything though you exceed £50. A knowledge of the value of
gums would be useful.

With respect to the paper for drying plants you will do well to consult Dr Hooker[5] and make that a separate item. Let me know as soon as possible. I shall submit it to Captain Washington the Hydrographer[6] who has a general superintendance of our expenses. Take a sufficient supply by all means and of corr. sublimate any quantity, (I have seen a smoothing iron used with great effect in drying plants in humid weather). The only difficulty I fear is transport up the river as our steam launch carries very little being only 80 feet by 8 ft. If we get up to Tette in the vessel that takes us out then we can deposit the heavier luggage there. Everything ought perhaps to be packed in two portions. We require to take as little as possible of dead weight consistent with efficiency.

What do you propose as necessary for collecting fruits and seeds. The animal kingdom & fishes are very interesting. I shall meet all your views as far as I can, so write freely. The Commission will be a general one and following the suggestions of the Royal Society and Geographical Societies will direct our attention to various departments.

I am etc Faithfully Yours
David Livingstone

I shall answer the other points as soon as possible. Kindest regards to my friend Professor Wilson. Tell him I am longing for a half hour to go and call on Playfair's new wife!

4

15 Whitehall Place
January 22nd, 1858

My Dear Sir,

On consulting Captain Washington about the paper for drying plants, he informed me that he has got five reams of it ready for you. He thinks that after you have made the list complete, it ought to be sent to the medical department of the Navy and that the medicines should be furnished by them – so if you have not already ordered any, you had better just send me the list and if you should come to London, you could see to the packing of them as you desire.

If convenient, it would be well for you to see Captain Washington before we go. He likes to be *acknowledged* and is also very useful in getting anything for you in his power. A quarter or half year's salary may be obtained. Hoping that this is not too late for reversing my decision about getting the medicines in Edinburgh.

I am etc
David Livingstone

Please name arsenical soap, corrosive sublimate etc in your list.

5

50 Albemarle Street
January 26th, 1858

My Dear Sir,

Your name was handed to me by Lord Clarendon with the statement that you were highly recommended by Sir William[7] and Dr Hooker, and also by Professors Balfour[8] and Wilson. It was approved by Lord Clarendon and sent by the Foreign Office to the Admiralty which has the further organisation of the Expedition. You are therefore *appointed* and all that is necessary now is that you present yourself to Captain Washington, the Hydrographer, for approval in that department, but no objection will be made.

It will be well if you lose no time in making preparations as to outfit, as we expect to be off about the 14th of February.

Thanks for the list. I shall order the packing according to your desire, but it would have been an advantage had you been at hand to see that it was attended to.

I am Yours Most Truly
David Livingstone

6

Manchester
January 28th, 1858

My Dear Sir,
   Your salary will commence on the 1st February and should you want more than a quarter's advance, I shall be obliged if you let me know. Don't leave your friends in any hurry on account of that. If you can get your things better where you are than in London, by all means do so – and you can remit the money afterwards. We must get all into trim by the 15th.
   Anything that I can get for you, please let me know and if possible I shall do my best to comply with your wishes – the amount of luggage has to be limited, but we shall try and make each other as comfortable as possible.

I am etc
David Livingstone

I shall be in London on Saturday.

7

18 Hart Street
February 17th, 1858

My Dear Sir,

I have not yet heard whether any arrangement was made for a Ward's case from Kew. I mentioned it to you but the subject may have escaped your memory. If we cannot have one from Kew we can apply elsewhere. I have got another parcel of seeds from Rollisson of Tooting and have forwarded them to Birkenhead. Those I gave in charge to you are, I believe, still at the Royal Geographical Society's house.

You will oblige me if you purchase some tincture of myrrh and keep it carefully for the Commandant of Tette,[9] who desired me to bring something for fastening loose teeth! If you know anything better or anything of an anodyne nature for his perineum, we may get on the soft side of him. I will repay you.

I am
Yours truly
David Livingstone

8

London
February 22nd, 1858

My Dear Sir,

From the present information we have of the sailing of
the *Pearl*[10] it will be necessary to be at Liverpool on Saturday next to prepare for sailing. Should any other information reach me, I will not fail to let you know.

Have we got a peach and apricot tree in the W. cases and
a vine or two. These seem very necessary.

I am going this afternoon to Glasgow, 4 Athol Place, but
do not write if you have got them.

I am etc
David Livingstone

9

Glasgow
February 28th, 1858

My Dear Sir,

The *Pearl* will sail from Greenock on Monday next and you will be expected at Liverpool on Tuesday in order to be ready for embarcation.

I am etc
David Livingstone

Some things require to be done to the *Pearl* at Liverpool. I enclose a note for your consideration. Glycerine is, I understand, good for preserving specimens.

10

Screw Steamship *Pearl*
at Sea off Madeira
March 18th, 1858

Dr John Kirk

Sir,

The main object of the Expedition to which you are appointed Economic Botanist and Medical Officer is to extend
the knowledge already attained of the geography and mineral
and agricultural resources of Eastern and Central Africa, to
improve our acquaintance with the inhabitants and to engage them to apply their energies to industrial pursuits and
to the cultivation of their lands with a view to the production of raw material to be exported to England in return for
British manufactures; and it may be hoped that by encouraging the natives to occupy themselves in the development
of the resources of their country a considerable advance may
be made towards the extinction of the slave trade, as the
natives will not be long in discovering that the former will
eventually become a more certain source of profit than the
latter.

2. It is intended that the Expedition should pass through
the malarious district at the lower portion of the Zambesi
river as quickly as possible, and it will be necessary for you
to put into practice those precautionary measures against

fever by the use of Quinine which the experience of the Niger Expedition, and your own judgement may suggest as likely to secure the health of your companions.

3. The efforts of every member of the Expedition will probably be required to facilitate the transport of the luggage to and beyond Tette, the most advanced post of civilization, but the chief power in the country adjacent being in the hands of two or three influential chiefs, it will be our duty to visit them and invite them to turn the attention of their people to the cultivation of cotton, by giving them a supply of better seed than that which they already possess, and also to explain the benefit that they would derive from an exchange of the natural productions of Africa, as ivory, cotton, oil, beeswax, buaze, etc. for the manufactures of Europe, and generally to hold out every encouragement in order to induce them to give up their warlike and predatory habits and substitute the more peaceable pursuits of agriculture and commerce. The time occupied in attending to these matters will enable you, if you find it to be consistent with your personal safety, to glean a general idea of the resources of the country to the North of Tette and to ascertain, in as full detail as the time will allow, the nature of the plant called Buaze, paying particular attention to the probable amount to which it and any other fibrous substances might be obtained. You will be good enough to furnish me with a Report thereon for transmission home to the Foreign Office.

4. Your attention is particularly requested to the discovery of dye stuffs, gums, and medicinal substances, in the hope that should either these or fibrous tissues exist in quantities sufficient to warrant commercial enterprise, you may aid in the great work of supplanting by lawful commerce the odious traffic in slaves. It is gratifying to me to feel assured

that this object commends itself to your mind as a most important and noble one, and I have the pleasure of handing you a copy of a sketch of the principal duties expected of you in the botanical department, drawn up by that eminent traveller and Botanist, Dr J. D. Hooker, whose success in reflecting honour on our country I heartily wish you may equal, and requesting, for this part of our travels at least, your earnest and exclusive attention to the same. Other objects of interest will no doubt press on your notice, but considering that the botany of this region is nearly unexplored – that there is a danger of over-working yourself – that your energies will be greater in the second than in the first year – and that the primary objects of the expedition are to gain accurate information respecting the vegetable and mineral resources of the country, I trust you will see the propriety of limiting, for a time, the range of your pursuits.

5. Our stay in the vicinity of Tette must necessarily be short because it is essential to proceed at an early period to the rapid, Kebrabasa or Chicova, to ascertain the possibility of passing it while the river is still comparatively high and thus avoid the necessity of taking the launch to pieces for porterage. The people near the Portuguese settlements who have been in contact with slave traders, not being so trustworthy as those further inland who have not been subjected to the prejudicial influence of such communication, it will be unadvisable to make any distant excursions. Our energies must be bent to the establishment of a depot at some eligible spot beyond the confluence of the Kafue and Zambesi. Having reached a tolerable elevation and examined the country adjacent, it will be advisable, after obtaining the consent of any natives who may lay claim to the soil, to set up the iron house to serve as a central station. As the spot selected will probably be on the side of one of the hills

which flank the river and sufficiently high to secure salubrity, a small plot of ground may at that altitude be planted with wheat and European vegetables as an experiment, and also in order to promote the comfort and health of the Expedition; while another small spot at a lower level may be planted with cotton and sugar cane, and given in charge to the headman of any village adjacent, in order to induce the natives to take an interest in the result.

6. The central depot once established and intercourse with the natives set on foot, a more extended range of scientific observation will then be advisable. You may then follow out as opportunity offers the instructions on Zoology from Professor Owen, contained in Appendix No. 2, and without discarding your botanical labours, collect any new or rare animals, birds, fishes or insects that may be met with in excursions which in company with the Makololo may safely be made, and the results be deposited at the central station.

7. Although these explorations and collections are very desirable, you will understand that Her Majesty's Government attach more importance to the moral influence which may be exerted on the mind of the natives by a well regulated and orderly household of Europeans setting an example of consistent moral conduct to all who may congregate around the settlement – treating the people with kindness and relieving their wants – teaching them to make experiments in agriculture – explaining to them the more simple arts – imparting to them religious instruction as far as they are capable of receiving it – and inculcating peace and good will to each other.

8. One especial means of gaining their favour will be by giving them the benefit of your medical skill and remedial aid. They possess medical men among themselves who are generally the most observant people to be met with. It is

desirable to be at all times on good terms with them. In order to do this, slight complaints, except among the very poor ought to be referred to their care, and severe cases before being undertaken should be enquired into of the doctor himself and no disparaging remark ever made on the previous treatment in the presence of the patient. This line of conduct will lead to the more urgent cases only being referred to you; time and medicine will both be saved, while your influence will be extended. Never neglect the opportunity which the bed of sickness presents of saying a few kind words in a natural respectful manner and imitate in as far as you can the conduct of the Great Physician, whose followers we profess to be.

9. The Expedition is well supplied with arms and ammunition and it will be necessary at times to use these in order to obtain supplies of food, as well as specimens of animals for the purposes of natural history. In many parts of the country which we hope to traverse, the larger animals exist in great numbers and being comparatively tame may be easily secured. I would earnestly press on you the duty of a sacred regard to life and never to destroy it, unless some justifiable end is to be answered by its extinction. The most vital part ought to be aimed at, and no shot fired unless the animal be within a range that renders it probable that the mortal part will be struck. The wanton waste of animal life which I have witnessed from night hunting and from the ferocious but child-like abuse of instruments of destruction, as well as the wish that the habits of certain races of animated creation, which are evidently destined at no very distant date to extinction, should be calmly and philosophically observed while there remains the opportunity, make me anxious that none of my companions should be guilty of similar abominations.

10. It is hoped we may never have occasion to use our arms for protection from the natives, but the best security from attack consists in upright conduct and the natives seeing that we are prepared to meet it. At the same time you are strictly enjoined to exercise the utmost forbearance towards the people, and while retaining proper firmness in the event of any misunderstanding, to conciliate as far as possibly can be admitted with safety to our own party.

11. It is unnecessary for me to enjoin the strictest justice in dealing with the people. This your own principles will lead you invariably to follow, but it is decidedly necessary to be careful not to *appear* to over reach or insult anyone. Care must be taken in every case in which a native is to be employed that the terms be well understood and a little patience in settling the amount of the remuneration in the presence of witnesses and the exact number of persons engaged will prevent that heart burning and discontent which otherwise may ensue. Let the payment be invariably made into the hands of the man who has performed the work. Unless this is done, the idea of property in the labour of the lower classes of the population is apt to be engendered in the minds of the under chiefs, but by direct payment a most important doctrine is widely inculcated and in process of time each man comes to feel that he owes subjection to the head chief alone and is otherwise a free subject.

12. The chiefs of tribes and leading men of villages ought always to be treated with great respect and nothing should be done to weaken their authority. Any present of food should be accepted frankly. It is impolitic to allow the ancient custom of feeding strangers to go into disuse. We come among them as members of a superior race, and servants of a Government that desires to elevate the more degraded portions of the human family. We are also

adherents of a holy benign religion and may by wise, patient efforts be the harbingers of peace to a hitherto distracted and trodden down race. No great result is ever obtained without patient and long continued efforts. In this enterprise in which we have the honour to be engaged, sympathy, consideration and kindness which when viewed in detail may seem thrown away if steadily persisted in, are sure ultimately to exercise a commanding influence. Depend upon it, a kind word or deed is never lost.

13. You will have access to Koelle's Poly Glotta Africana, Bleek's vocabulary of the languages of Mosambique and an Analysis of the Sechuana tongue, and you are to endeavour to master the latter language as it is generally spoken in the Makololo country and its acquisition will materially aid you in all your pursuits. Should opportunity offer, you are expected to collect vocabularies of other dialects, using the system already employed in the Sechuana – taking the English consonants and giving the vowels the sound they have in Italian, Spanish and in most European languages.

14. You are distinctly to understand that your services are engaged for two years, unless any unforseen accident should happen to the Expedition, when you will be set free as soon as an opportunity is afforded for returning to England.

15. In the event of my being prostrated by illness or by accident, rendered incapable of conducting the Expedition, the charge of it will devolve on Commander Bedingfeld. If he too should fail, it will devolve on you and then on Mr Charles Livingstone, but immediate information of such an event is, if possible, to be transmitted to England for further instructions.

16. You are at liberty to consult a copy of the original instructions I hold from Her Majesty's Government, and it

is hoped that you will enter cordially into the spirit of them and so far as circumstances will allow, endeavour to carry them into effect.

17. Finally, you are strictly enjoined to take the greatest care of your own health and that of the Expedition. My own experience teaches the necessity of more than ordinary attention to the state of the alimentary canal – constipation is almost sure to bring on fever – and it would be well if you kindly explain to the different members the necessity of timely remedial aid to overcome any tendency to it, especially if accompanied by dreaming, drowsiness, want of appetite or unpleasant taste in the mouth in the mornings. If Quinine combined with a mild aperient be administered, this precautionary measure will often ward off an attack of this formidable disease. Feeling the fullest confidence in your zeal in the great cause of African civilisation and rejoicing in being associated with you in this noble work, I heartily commit you and the cause in which you will, I hope, be an influential Pioneer, to the safe keeping of the Almighty Disposer of events.

I am your
Most Obedient Servant
David Livingstone

British Museum
January 12th, 1858

Duties of Botanist
1. To ascertain exactly the species and varieties of plants in cultivation among the natives and colonists, for all purposes; preserving good herbarium specimens of these in leaf,

flower, and when possible, in fruit, accompanying them with notes; and to preserve dried or in spirits, the larger fruits, cereals etc for exhibition in the Museum of Economic Botany at Kew. It is probable that a full investigation of such products will demonstrate the capabilities of the country for increased cultivation and, since East African vegetables are known to be, with a few exceptions, commonly cultivated in India, the climate and resources of the several districts in the latter country being approximately known, a safe standard of comparison will be obtained, upon which to base conclusions as to the manner in which the vegetable resources of Eastern Africa may best be further developed.

2. To ascertain exactly the indigenous plants yielding food, clothing, medicinal products, timber, ornamental wood, gums, resins, oils, dye stuffs etc; to procure good herbarium specimens of them in leaf, flower and fruit, accompanied with specimens of the woods (which should bear the same numbers as the dried specimens branded or stamped upon them) and of other products of all kinds, for experiment and exhibition in England.

With regard to such plants and their products, their value may in certain cases be ascertained upon the spot; thus a well instructed scientific man of careful habits of observation, may by cautious experiments in the case of medicinal products and with the aid of a few chemical preparations in the case of dye stuffs etc either at once obtain conclusive results or be led to direct his attention to the investigation of allied plants.

3. Though considerable practical results may be expected from the attention of a skilled observer being directed to the above points of enquiry in a field so novel and teeming with vegetable life, yet the Committee of the Royal Society

consider that the material objects of this department of the East African Expedition cannot be fully carried out, except the person charged with these duties be impressed with the importance of thoroughly investigating scientifically, the climate and vegetation and of ascertaining the laws that regulate the exuberance of the latter and the reasonable chances there may be of replacing it by introduced plants. They would advert to the fact that the introduction of tea, coffee, indigo, oats and other most important recently introduced vegetable products into India, was due to the recommendation of experienced men of high scientific attainments (Sir Joseph Banks, Sir William Jones, Drs Wright, Royle, Wallich, Falconer, etc.) whose experiments almost invariably proved successful, while innumerable similar attempts of uninstructed persons, however powerfully supported, have failed.

Now it is generally supposed that the regions to which Dr Livingstone is proceeding, are well adapted to the cultivation of indigo, cotton, coffee, rice, spices, sugar, etc. only because the favourable conditions of the climate and soil are manifest; but it must not be forgotten that unfavourable conditions, if any, are in such circumstances, as always, hidden and subtil; often depending on the relative abundance and vigour of the native vegetation, which in all countries interposes a formidable obstacle to the introduction of cultivated plants. It is hence most important both in this, and other inquiries of the same nature, that the Botanist should make a full collection of the native plants of every kind, with notes of their localities, general abundance and distribution; for an accurate investigation of these will afford to himself the surest foundation on which to base his conclusions and will enable many who cannot visit the country to suggest plans for its amelioration.

This is the more necessary because, owing to the novelty,

luxuriance, and variety of a tropical vegetation, it is impossible for any Botanist, however skilled and learned, to obtain a definite idea of its real nature, except he not only observe each vegetable form, but makes a record of it in the shape of a specimen. Every effort should, therefore, be made by the expedition towards the formation of a complete herbarium, for reasons quite independent of its scientific value.

(Signed) Joseph D. Hooker

=======

Instructions to the Zoologist of the Zambesi Expedition

1. *Tsetse Fly* (Glossina Morsitans)

The most important practical question demanding the attention of the Zoologist of the Zambesi Expedition is the Natural history of the Tsetse fly (Glossina morsitans). The alleged fatal effects of this insect in the case of oxen and horses subject to its bites, should be determined with the utmost possible precision in regard to the number of bites or punctures occasioning death, the previous state of health of the animal bitten, the temperature, locality and other external conditions coincident with the wounds and their fatal result. It should first be determined whether one or more kinds of fly have been designated by the term 'tsetse' and if this is restricted to the *Glossina morsitans*; next whether any other species of insect produces similar effects on animals in the Zambesi district.

From the concurrent testimony of travellers in South Africa, it appears that the presence of the Tsetse fly is a barrier to progress by means of oxen and horses through the districts infected by it. The tsetse fly would prove a similar or greater obstacle to a settlement in the so infested districts, by any colony depending upon cattle or horses for food or transport. The extirpation of the species will most probably require the same kind of entomological knowledge and investigation as those which have been elicited by the rewards and prizes proposed by Agricultural Associations in reference to the extirpation of particular species of noxious insects destructive of agricultural products in this country – the Turnip Flea etc.

This essential preliminary kind of knowledge as guiding to the right or best steps for the riddance of the tsetse fly in the districts of the Zambesi infested by it, will include: the period and place of its oviposition; the nature and course of its metamorphosis; the habitats of the larva and pupa; the ordinary food and period of existence of the insect in its perfect state; in short, as complete a Natural History of it as the time and opportunities for observation and experiment may allow to be carried out by the Zoologist of the expedition. Any alleged remedy for the poisoning of the tsetse; any application reported by natives to be attended with success, should be experimented with, when opportunity offers, and the precise nature of the remedial product should be determined.

2. Ivory

The commercial value of ivory, the alleged large proportional size of the tusks and fine quality of the Ivory supplied by the elephants of the Zambesi district, render all that relates to it and can be accurately ascertained respecting the food, haunts and habits of that variety of elephant an object of great practical importance; especially in a consideration of the increasing scarcity and price of Ivory during the last half of the century.

The sexual distinction of the tusks should be carefully

noted by comparison of male and female Elephants of different ages.

If the teeth of one side of the lower jaw be preserved with the tusks of each elephant killed for the sake of the ivory, data for determining the rate of growth of the tusks will be, for the first time, collected.

In the event of a female elephant being killed in the pregnant state, the uterus and foetus should, if possible, be preserved in a keg of spirit, according to the instructions to be afterwards referred to.

Among the best means of determining whether the large tusked Zambesi Elephants are specifically distinct from, or a variety of the more Southern African Elephants, a series of grinding teeth from the first small one developed in the sucking Elephant to the last or largest grinder in the oldest Elephant, should be collected.

3. *Lepidosiren*

The attention of the Naturalist should be especially directed to the probable existence of Lepidosireus in the Zambesi. By examining mud banks which may be left dry during the hot and dry season and by digging round any hole leading vertically into the mud, a species, perhaps nondescript, of that anomalous genus may be detected and captured in its torpid state. For the preservation of such specimens and for that of animals generally, the 'Instructions' under the head 'Zoology' printed in the Admiralty Manual for collecting and observing, of which a copy is annexed, will probably meet all the requirements, under this head, of the Naturalist of the Zambesi Expedition.

(signed) Richard Owen

11

Pearl
April 15th, 1858

Private

My Dear Sir,

In handing to you the accompanying letter of instructions,[11] I may be allowed to suggest that when you write the
report required, you will do it as carefully as possible, as I
intend to send your own manuscript to the Foreign Secretary. I think that it is my duty to promote the interests of
my companions as far as lies in my power, and by thus
bringing you as it were into direct contact with the Government, it may ultimately tend to your benefit. If you make it
as clear and simple as possible, it will secure attention.

I shall try and get your plants home to Dr Hooker, as
soon as possible, as it is of importance to get them into the
hands of our friend before the German of Angola.[12]

> Believe me yours
> most truly
> David Livingstone

12

off Shupanga
July 21st, 1858

My Dear Dr Kirk, etc.,

We came to Mazaro this morning about 9½ and, on going ashore among a crowd of natives and Portuguese, were sickened by the sight of headless mutilated bodies lying about. The Governor having fever, the officers begged me to take him on to Shupanga. I consented and while waiting for him the firing began a short distance off. Everything was in confusion and the commandant of Tette and Mr Azevedo and Colonel Nuñez[13] all told me that the man at Shupanga was a thief and would connive at the Landeens[14] robbing us of the goods we intended to leave. It seems therefore decidedly necessary for us to go on to Senna. It would be throwing them away here. We shall be three days to that place now that we know the way.

My Dear Friends you must exercise patience. I would remain at the island myself but feel my presence necessary when either natives or Portuguese come to us, to make our objects understood. If you see any plan by which we might hasten our departure from the island, let me know when I come down. I still think the Portuguese may help us, but war engrosses every thought. I go ashore here to try and get some fowls sent down to you. Examine all the things and use by all means everything you like. I forgot to say, before

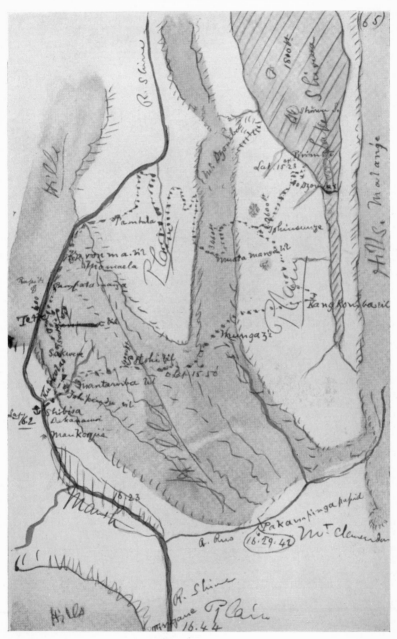

A sketch map of the Shire Highlands by Kirk, 1859.

leaving, that you ought to make fresh bread for yourselves. The flour is under my boxes. God bless and preserve you all. Baines is quite well now. May I suggest a short morning prayer again. We have been unable to attend to this for some time past.

My kindest salutations to you all
David Livingstone

13

Island of Pita, above Senna
August 25th, 1858

My Dear Dr Kirk,

I send this in order to let you know that we have been obliged to alter our plan so far as to leave the Pinnace here in charge of Mr Baines. We reached Senna in four days being the shortest voyage made though the water is now getting very shoal and we had a whale boat overturned by the paddle, Tom, Will and Peter moving it aft while we were going though I told them I should stop to allow them to do so. We lost thereby the box of plants and some iron things. The casks floated and were all recovered. Toby was nearly carried away by the current, he having jumped in to save things and Tom Jumbo nobly saved him. We spent part of two days at Senna, then came on with two pilots who have led us into difficulties several times. In going into doubtful places it is necessary to go slowly – the Pinnace catches first and the slightest touch makes the Launch shew her want of power by slewing round. Three times she has done that with me (Bedingfeld[15] did it often) and when she goes on a shoal, the current keeps her on and much time is lost. We lightened the Pinnace as much as possible into the Launch but still she draws so much as to be a great hindrance. Baines volunteered to remain with her and I declined as one of the objects I had in view was to get him up to Tette, but having lost a whole day by Jumbo not having the anchor ready when she began to slew round, I see it is absolutely necessary to make a trial trip in the Launch first and then, when we know the river, take the Pinnace. Please to speak about these matters to Thornton only. Bedingfeld will chuckle over any of our difficulties and make more of them than a truthful man would. He may possibly try, by misrepresentation, to prevent our getting any fresh grant for what we shall need. As I mention his name, I may on this occasion state that H. M.'s Government in order to prevent insubordination, such as Baikie[16] suffers from on the Niger Expedition, invested me with magisterial power as a consul, expressly to meet such a case as Bedingfeld's. I find from the document purporting to be a Log kept on board the *Ma Robert* which you delivered to me, that he trusts in the power of re-iterated assertion to prove my harshness etc, etc. I return the document as evidence and will require you to certify having got it from him as a Log for the satisfaction of the Foreign Secretary of State. As I must give a full statement of the whole affair to the Foreign Office, I shall require your (medical) evidence as to the state of filth in which, on taking charge of the *Ma Robert*, we found the decks, as I considered it prejudicial to health and long before that recommended him to adopt a regular system of cleaning them. As also in respect to his having told you that he

had given in to me a second resignation, and as you are
now the second in command, your opinion expressed to me,
when I shewed you my acceptance of that resignation, that
it was absolutely necessary to save the expedition from
complete disorganisation or words to that effect, would
prove of no ordinary value to the Foreign Secretary from an
impartial witness, for whom alone the evidence is required.
It goes to him direct and is not published. As B. seems
disposed to make something out of your signing a paper, I
think it would be well to state also how much he asked and
how much you meant in doing so. He refers to it in two
documents. I am not conscious of anything disagreeable or
harsh in my conduct nor have I been quarrelsome with anyone and in sending evidence to the Foreign Office, I do so
with extreme regret and sorrow that public duty requires it
to be done against any of our number. I earnestly hope and
pray that nothing may arise to disturb the harmony which
has hitherto existed among the rest of us.

Baines is much better and has been working at everything
in which he could be useful. Black Will is bilious. Mr Rae
is better but a little shaken. Mr L. was second engineer
when R. was down. Coffee thought himself the first. The
Kroomen[17] all work admirably. They cut as much wood in
one hour as they used to do in four. Can you give Major
Sicard [18] a little black tea as he says it is diuretic.

Ever yours
David Livingstone

Should you be desirous of getting away before I come and
can arrange with the Portuguese to take you and a cargo for
say £20 or £25, pray dont hesitate.

14

Dakana Moro Island,
River Shire
October 17th, 1859

Dr Kirk

Sir,

You are hereby required to pass overland with Mr Rae to Tette in order to bring away two persons, lately members of this Expedition, in order to send them home by the Man of War appointed to meet us at Kongone Harbour in the middle of November next.

As Mr Thornton, one of the persons referred to, has been honest, and failed in his duties as geologist chiefly from ignorance and a want of energy, he is permitted to take the geological specimens with him but on the understanding that they are Government property and must be handed over to the Geological Society when required. He must give you an acknowledgement in writing to that effect. Otherwise, they are to be retained at Tette.

The other individual, Mr Baines, referred to, having been guilty of gross breaches of trust in *secretly* making away with large quantities of public property, and having been in the habit of secreting Expedition property in his private boxes, it will be necessary for you to examine his boxes (after ascertaining whether my order to him to deliver up to

Major Sicard all paintings, drawings and other public property, has been complied with) the more especially as he had only three *private* boxes in his possession on leaving the *Pearl* and these are now increased by the appropriation of 'biscuit boxes' to which he has no right – no permission having ever been asked or granted.

It will be proper for you to ask him in the presence of Mr Rae, what he did with five jars of butter which he took out of a cask and never sent to table or for cooking. What he did with five barrels of Loaf sugar which he was seen opening and drying but were never used in the Expedition. The answers to these and other questions to be put down in the storekeeper's book as soon as convenient and signed by yourself and Mr Rae. Take possession of this book – of another book of mine in his boxes, *The Plant* – specimens of brass rings and of everything else you have reason to believe does not belong to him. If he declines your offer of conveyance, he is left to his own resources.

I am etc
David Livingstone

15

Shamoara[19]
October 29th, 1859

My Dear Dr Kirk,

We left Chibisa's on the 25th after completing the magnetical observations. We were at Morambala last night but a storm which continued all night prevented our seeing the occultation. I hope you were more fortunate.

Supposing you to be at Tette last night, I have resolved to send up Rowe[20] to get a box of biscuits and a jar of butter at Senna, while the men who remain cut wood here – and when we get a load and Rowe has returned, we shall go down to Shupanga and wait for you there. We have got several blows in coming down. We were driven right ashore by the wind last night and hurt our paddles. We make more water than when you left too – so the sooner she is in dock the better. Rowe will bring the mail if you have not come down quicker than we expected and got them.

My brother has had fever again and badly – compliments to Rae.

D. Livingstone

I have told Ferrão that there are many large Lakes like seas, north of Tette and Burton[21] has discovered them. We have been to Nyassa or Nyinyesi and it was very hot. If Rowe and Hutchins have not reached Senna, then be good enough to bring butter and salt and a box of flour and one tin biscuits, as we may have but one.

16

November 3rd, 1859

Dr Kirk,

We found several letters for Dr Kirk, Mr Thornton and one for Mr Rae but keep them in the Launch lest they pass you on the road. We leave for Shupanga tomorrow 4th. Have a lot of Buaze in flower drying. We are all well now. I think Knapp's *Technology* has come.

D. L.

17

Shupanga
November 6th, 1859

My Dear Dr Kirk,

You will no doubt be disappointed at not finding us here
– but there is no help for it as we are sinking. We waited at
Shamoara till yesterday morning (5th). We had made a
good deal of water and had to pump during the night while
Rowe was away – but lying in a still place the leak seemed
to fill up. As you did not make your appearance, I resolved
to run down here for food for the crew and went to bed last
night all right. In the morning, we found the right-hand
after hold and forehold as well as stoke hole with a large
quantity of water. This is in addition to the constant leak
where the men sleep. Tried to stop the leak in after hold
and failed. We have to pump every little while. The only
chance of saving her is to get her beached without loss of
time. We are therefore cutting wood today and will run
down tomorrow to Kongone. I leave a whaler for you. You
must just do the best you can in the case. I leave your letters
– one torn, you will see how. We have a small square box
or tin for you besides. My brother is better.

David Livingstone

I am hard up for paper you see.

18

Cataracts
June 2nd, 1863

My Dear Dr Kirk,

Moloka returned from Senna yesterday with four bulls, four cows and two calves, and I have written to Col. Nuñez. If you have sufficient money to pay Mr Ferrão, would you do it? If you find that the other orders swallow up most of the £150 from the Cape, be good enough to draw £50 or a £100, according to the paper I gave you and leave what you can in Col. Nuñez' hands.

I am as thin as yourself, having got the turn fairly about 29th ult. I still have the discharge of pus you laboured under. Meller[22] had it, but a thorough good sharp rousing out cured it at once, the peculiar pain above and behind the bladder leaving him at once. We are all in better health – the weather having quite changed – air 49° this morning.

The missionaries are pretty well. Proctor[23] and Waller[24] went across the plain in front on a terribly wet day, which you too probably caught or was caught by, turned and came back drenched. Went again but Proctor became ill about Mbames and had to be brought home. Proctor is still seedy and bilious. We have two carpenters from Senna and are making paddle floats. I shall not be able to start for a week yet as I am very weak.

Rae tells me that Mr Stewart[25] went away saying he had seen only 5 cotton bushes in the whole country and no indigo. The fact seems to be, if the saying is true, he did not know either the one or the other, for there are a good many cotton bushes within a stone cast of Shupanga house, around the huts of the natives and no end of indigo. Here in the neuk along which we lie, I went and counted seventy seven cotton bushes. Waller saw only one – but more than that, along the very path Mr S. came, there are at least 3 acres in one spot. I mean to count the bushes by the path against which Mr Stewart rubbed his clothes and suspect they will come nearer 500 than 5. It is a pity that he did not speak to either of us while at Shupanga. We could have shewn the difference between having eyes and being able to use them.

I am sure I wish you every success in your future life. You were always a right hand to me and I never trusted you in vain. God bless and prosper you.

If you see my boy Robert,[26] say a kind word to him and advise him to work, for I fear he may turn out a 'Ne'er do weel'.

> I am yours with sincere
> Affection
> David Livingstone

Some Ajawa expelled from the Makololo went down near Mankokwes – made war – killed a headman and plundered the gardens. After expulsion they hovered about the Mission for some weeks, and now one Makololo after another comes to them condoling with the brethren that *Mission people* should have acted so badly!!

19

Cataracts of Shire
July 5th, 1863

My Dear Dr Kirk,

The new Bishop[27] came up to us yesterday and I received the Despatch containing our recall the day before. The time appointed for us to be down at the mouth of the river is the end of this month and no salary is to be due after 31st December. This has not been unlooked for by me. It rather relieves my mind about the *Lady Nyassa* as we can screw her together and sell her in India. As you know, the Portuguese, by clearing off the population, finished our work but this is not adverted to in the recall – perhaps it would have been impolitic. The difficulties we encountered are adverted to, zeal and perseverance, etc., etc. praised, but the 'information we have given is rather scant' says his Lordship. Now you may go in on that to give a magnificent botanical work, economical and everything else, at Government expense – at least I mean to put that to him.

As we can't come down with *Pioneer* though we could with *Lady Nyassa*, I am going up to the North end of Lake Nyassa directly to improve the intermediate time. The Makololo[28] go with me. The boat was burned I think by accidental firing of the grass, and by, the Ajawa say, the Manganja – I don't believe them, as all the copper and iron lay untouched below.

J. Reid is better – a smart dose of calomel when Meller was down at the Mission cleared away spleen and everything else. I persuaded Meller to give the same to King and his haemorrhoids went apace. He was quite bloodless and delirious each night – but we took him up to Mokurumazi and he walked all the way home. This is all by way of increasing your medical knowledge! Proctor is ill and retires, Rowley[29] on his last legs. *They say*, too, Waller ill yesterday. The new Bishop a good cautious man, thinks of trying the top of Morambala. I am sure I welcome the new squad heartily, though Rowley and others would place all the blame of their fighting on me.

Teaching is to be the order of the day. He thinks it scandalous no effort has been made to convey Christian knowledge. He comes from the fens of Lincolnshire and ought to be enured to malaria. I take the black Whaler and wish you were with me again. Nearly all the Makololo go but stop at some point to hunt elephants, while I go on with five in the boat.

When Proctor's hut was burned, several guns going off made the Makololo think the Mission was attacked by an armed force. They at once rushed with spears, etc. to the rescue. This is per Blair. If correct, no fear need be entertained of them attacking the Mission. My son Robert is at Natal. Give him a kind word if you see him and may God bless you.

Yours with affection
David Livingstone

I received two Mazaro notes from you. Thanks. Sorry you missed *Orestes*.

20

1863?

. . .[30] On arriving at the Mission, please select any papers or articles likely to be valued by Mr Thornton's friends and take them if the canoe will admit them.

Be good enough to proceed with all convenient speed down the river and make enquiries of Tito or Bandeiro[31] or Vianna's[32] representative about sending up a canoe with 100 panjas of rice and Mexoeira. Tito said that he could furnish rice cheaper than anyone else and if he would undertake it, the business would be done better by him. Vianna charged more than double the ordinary price for grain and a canoe load cost, with canoe men and canoe, £21. It must be got even at that, but if it is to be had any cheaper, the sender will be quite as content, and we more.

The boat I should like to be employed to bring up whatever may be found for us but if nothing has been left or come from Mosambique, then it may have mexoeira or rice and a Shupanga crew of ten to serve six months, at a price per month to relieve those here, our former ones if possible. Any dispatches that may have arrived to be hastened up in Thornton's boat – by part of the ten Shupanga men I sent to the Cape for £150, to be left in Col. Nuñez' hands – pay Tito for 46 or 50 panjas of clean rice and anything else he may send, also £18 to Sr Manoel's[33] agent for the sheep and goats we received – or rather place the money in Sr Galdino's[34] hands, to be given on receipt of Mr Thornton's bill of exchange. Pay Ali and Mabruck at the rate of six dollars per month, for Ali, that is 5 of agreement and one of back-shish, and four dollars per month as per agreement (3 and 1 of backshish) and send the amount given in a note to Admiral Washington. The dates are from 21st March, 1862 to the probable arrival at Zanzibar.

Make urgent representations to the Captain of any Man of War as to the necessity of sending into Quillimane or Kongone a supply of provisions, and make any arrangements you can to have them sent up quickly. If necessary, write an official letter and on his refusal send a copy to the Foreign Office.

If there is any difficulty with Tito, try if Col. Nuñez will undertake to send rice, etc. and provisions and pay himself out of the money which is to be delivered to him, namely £150.

David Livingstone

The men belonging to the Navy who accompany you are to proceed to Quillimane and rationed there, until an opportunity occurs of going to Mosambique in search of a Man of War. They are on no account to be left at Quillimane and if necessary, to remain there any time, as much care of them taken as possible. They are to be delivered over to the Captain of the first cruizer met.

David Livingstone

21

Malango
August 8th, 1863

My Dear Dr Kirk,
  I received your welcome letters by the boat in the beginning of August instead of, as you thought, the middle. The
canoe with grain and sugar had still to come. You did all
that a man could do in the circumstances and I thank you
for your services – suspecting that the silly Cape Governor
had not sent the money which his predecessor, Sir George
Grey,[35] was always glad to do and indeed pressed me to
make use of him in that and every other way I could think
of. I gave Dr Meller a bill for £150 to Colonel Nuñez
instead, but you will be off by the time of his arrival and I
fear he may not go to Quillimane at all. You were quite
right to get off by the earliest safe opportunity – that dying
by inches – slow and sure poison which I saw in the crew of
a Hamburgh vessel, was just what you describe in Saunders.
Be sure and write when you get this and let me know how
you are yourself. I feel naturally very anxious about you and
the rest. Sorry for poor Pearce. I shall send off his packet as
soon as I can. We are, thanks to the Highest, all well except
King, who complains of pains in his limbs, but works.
  I have written a formal complaint against being subjected
to the humiliation of having our Dispatch subjected to missionary and other gossip at the Cape, before we knew its
contents. I suspect the Governor of the Cape is the guilty

person and after telling how Adams came up and hailed the ship with 'no more pay for you *Pioneer* chaps. I brings the letter as says it' and that Dr Steere[36] had expatiated on the different paragraphs before English and Portuguese at Quillimane, until you had felt compelled to the remark 'that it was not likely that he could know the contents, etc.' I add that notwithstanding the courteousness of its style, my companions and self had been subjected to very unmerited humiliation – the Dispatch was sent open to the Cape Governor and I suspect that he, to gain a little popularity with high church folks, had sent it to the bishop. I shall not call on the Governor, though I go to the Cape and will take further public notice of the indignity, if no apology is given. I don't say a word to the bishop about it but will mention Dr Steere's bad manners. Earl Russell[37] says 'he will be glad to learn that any of the gentlemen of the Mission have profited by my suggestions and experience', etc., etc. – as they know this, I shall use it as a text.

We liked the bishop well enough during his half day's stay with [us]. He is the picture of Dillon of the *Gorgon*, but marked with small pox – very cautious and no courage, but seems not too old to learn. He might as well have mentioned his decision about Morambala. As it was, he let me see that he was mainly anxious to get me to coincide in his own views and he did not conceal his intention to bolt. He gave a hint about pickings out of *Pioneer* but I shall take care that they be of the smallest and as for *Lady Nyassa*, I would rather see her forming a second bar at Quillimane than that she should be a slaver or Portuguese property, which would be the equivalent. We mean to take her to India when the hurricane season is over – wish we could get into the Webbe to wait for that.

Washington pointedly said 'On no account take any money from private persons for her' and he sanctioned

*The Lady Nyassa in process of construction, with the Pioneer
at Shupanga, June 1862. Photograph by Kirk.*

several things additional which come to a good sum, yet not a word is said about her. I am not going to whine about it however. In reference to the remark in the Dispatch that the Government as yet possessed but scanty information about the resources of the country – I mention the ample materials you have sent or taken to the Government Museum at Kew and that there is no instance on record of valuable information being arranged without consulting Herbaria and authorities – and refer to Sir William Hooker as to whether the materials are not as ample for the illustration of the natural productions of the country as ever came out of a barbarous country and from a vessel in which nothing, without incessant trouble, could be preserved. I write to Sir William at same time. I suspect some underling has suggested the remark, Sir Roderick seems no longer our friend, and he has a say in everything. I only conjecture Sir Roderick's coldness, from his ceasing to write.

Rae gets on very fast in re-building *Lady Nyassa*. His heart is in it.

The worthy Laird of Limefield[38] says that we must be awful 'clashers' out here. We surely must, as the 'clashers' got so far before reaching us on the spot. About a month ago we were talking just as we used to do about the Governor of Quillimane making so much of medical services to the army and auxiliary forces, without ever thanking me for conveying him out of the thick of it, when it suddenly struck me that this might, with additions, be converted into a 'clash' I never contemplated. If it does so become, you will know what to think of it. Meller left us on 17th July. He is spoken of as Consul for Madagascar and had applied for it. I don't know if anyone is appointed to Zanzibar but it might be well for you to apply. In a few years, you could retire with a competency and have done good service in the meantime.

Z.D.—F

Waller wished to retire rather than go to Morambala but the bishop gave in to taking the freed women and children and he will go. He would have been such a mule to sit on a mountain without people to teach. Proctor went down river very ill with liver and living in a low valley doing nothing. They have, it is said, brought a sickly lad with them, who will soon die and give an excuse for halting. I have told Earl Russell that the use made of my previous advice not to fight or engage in native quarrels, which Bishop Mackenzie[39] honestly mentions in his journal, was to place all the blame of their subsequent fighting on my shoulders. The mountain Morambala to which they now go, will subject them by its frequent clouds to chills and damps which may be as prejudicial as the fevers in the valley. They must not blame me for it. Rowley is better.

We left to carry a boat past the cataracts and improve the time between this and December. I had it up at Malango when in the water. The Makololo reported that it would require now to be carried. I called all hands to do this, when five Shupanga men – I must give the names of the worthies – Kanyai, Peoso, Arimasau, Ropa and Mandzu (the slave) jumped in to shew how clever they were. The next thing I saw was the boat bottom upwards away like a shot over the cataracts! I am going to do a little on foot to keep the blood circulating.

My son, Robert, is said to be at Natal to join me and I am sorry I cannot ask anyone save Captain Gardner[40] to give him a passage and he wont touch there. He would be useful in the *L. Nyassa* If you can drop a word about a passage to any likely skipper, I shall be obliged. If he cannot come, he must work his own way in Natal.

With best wishes
I am ever yours
David Livingstone

22

Murchison's Cataracts
December 9th, 1863

My Dear Dr Kirk,
   Your welcome letters of June – at Quillimane – at Mosambique – and at Johanna, were found by me on my arrival
– the last day of October and I thank you heartily for all the
trouble you took in giving me such a full account of every
thing. I dont see that affairs could have been managed better
and feel thankful that you are fairly off and in tolerable
health. I was very anxious about you all and often thought
of you during our tramp.
   Meller went to Kongone and was very ill (he got over it as
we hear, when he was at Mazaro, on his way to Mosambique with Rowley and Proctor, but was salinated[41]) so
much so indeed that the information received here leaves
room barely for hope. I am very sorry about it. He is reported to have pushed the canoe through the black slush of
Quillimane river at night with trowsers off and then became
so ill that he was carried out at Kongone to see a ship pass.
As we are pretty well accustomed to the awful in reports, I
try to comfort myself in thinking this must be taken *cum
grano salis* and that we shall hear a more favourable account
soon.
   Tito is a dirty little beast, and I am quite aware of his
leanings towards me. My refusal to make him a confidante

was a never to be forgotten sin. It was well just to let him rave and not kick him.

The Mission is, we hear, up on the top of Morambala about its middle – and have to keep up fires continually – the vapour condensing keeps dripping through the huts and everything rusts. The bishop took the boys, but refused the women and children on account of the missionaries all being of the opposite sex. They have none to teach but the boys. Waller has left them and is waiting a passage by us. He wont give up the women and children to be again taken by the Portuguese and I shall have to take them out of the way, to Johanna probably. I am sorry that Waller left the mission for now they will have to experience *de novo*, but I suspect the new party wished to get rid of the old. You are blamed for alleging that Waller broke the late bishop's crook, which set Dr Steere's back up. If the subject is mentioned, I shall take care and stand up for you. There seems to have been a good deal of petty mumbling going on and much said, as if from our table.

I told you of the loss of the boat. After it we went on foot and tried to get away N.W. from the Upper Cataracts but met a range of high mountains on the west of which lies the high Maravi country. The valley at the base was over 2,000 feet high – very beautiful and plenty of fine streams of delicious cold water. Misled by the statement that no people lived beyond the range, we went along the valley till we came out at the heel of Nyassa – struck N.W. again, intending to get to the Latitude of the end of the Lake, yet west of the Mazite but came to a stockade where Mazite had been the day before. Dead bodies shewed this to be true – so we turned away N.E. till we reached the shores of the Lake at Chitanda. At Kota Kota or Marengo's found the two Arabs we met before, building a new dhow. The old one had been wrecked. They were busy carrying slaves across in two boats.

Up to this point, the shores of the Lake were one continued village of fugitives and the Arabs were buying as fast as they could, at one fathom for a boy and two for a girl. We then went due West on the great slave route to Katanga, the Babisa[42] and Cazembe's. After climbing up to what seems a range of high hills from below, we were on a level plain with a delicious air. We went in round numbers about 90 miles West, then turned up to the North but our time was spent. We must be back by the beginning of November and now we are into December, and no rise of the river. I might have speculated on a late flood but we had much sickness, and dysentery doubled me up nearly. A Lake called Bemba was reported 10 days N.N.W. and other lakes mentioned. The watershed clearly Westwards – Here rises the Loangwa of the Lake and close to it the Loangwa of the Maravi, which joins the Zambesi at Zumbo. No large river can enter Nyassa in the North and indeed the numbers of running streams I crossed, whose mouths choked with reeds we did not see from the boat, make it likely that one large river [?] is not necessary to account for the Shire. Two small ones do enter beyond where we formerly turned. The climate is humid, as seen by the trees covered with Lichens, as at the Kongone – vegetation stunted – villages of Babisa and Manganja very numerous and much cultivation carried on. Food dear, and I believe, though the slaves are so cheap, without ivory the trade would be unprofitable. They carry it and are often bought for this very purpose. The Shupanga men, who are malaria proof in the Delta, succumbed on the heights – and one of them actually died from change of air. The temperature was not low. They complained of pains all over – cut themselves everywhere, I never saw anything like it. They were useless – this too had some effect in causing them to return. I had the Steward with me, because all deprecated my going alone. He walked well and came back all right. Found that all had enjoyed very good health here in my absence – better in fact than when they had medical attendance and medical comforts! *Lady Nyassa* all ready to go down if the water rises. Rae well and doing well. King has swelled legs of late. Waller lives down at Marambala apart. The Mission Ajawa stole Mankokwe's maize and cleverly put the blame on the Makololo, but one was shot by Mankokwe's people in the act. Waller sent for an Ajawa chief in the hills by way of saving his own folks from the terrible Makololo, in his absence. He (the chief) came again and joined his countrymen against Mankokwe but got the worst of it. Then a larger party was sent for from the hills and with them went the Makololo against Mankokwe, who escaped on to the island. We went round in the *Pioneer* – the Ajawa live on the left bank now and the Makololo on the right. The former came up to me with a long story about Moloka's wife. I asked what the woman wished – does she wish to go back? This ended one of Waller's interminable 'Milalidos'. They have said no more about it. Mariano[43] is dead but first sent to the mission, giving notice that they were on his ground! Disease is same as Isidores. His people are selling off all his captives and slaving is going on fast and furious.

P.S. 17th Water not yet up. We hope for it at full moon on 24th. I received a note from the bishop, saying he 'had determined to leave the Zambesi as early in the coming year as possible' and had written to Captain Gardner to help him away. As well go as do nothing, we sent up six boys and gave Blair strict injunctions not to take them to the ship. They were put ashore at Chisiba's without anything. Of the rest, he has let the Portuguese know that if demanded he will give them up. This is Blair's story and I don't know what of it to believe. Dr Steere is everything and he is seedy from long drenching in clouds. When a cloud comes over them, they must run into the huts or be wetted to the skin and all the clouds come to them! The bishop sent us some wine, brandy, flour and sugar, which was very good of him. Offers more, as he is going, but I hope to be away as soon as he. I suspect that he will make tracks for the capital of Madagascar, where all the hard work has been done by other men – but it is only conjecture.

The Governor of Tette's wife and daughter are dead and I am murdered up at the Lake, no mistake this time – the new Governor de Portugal has arrived at Quillimane. A Johanna man, he who wore shoes on account of sores in the soles of his feet, was taken off by a crocodile at the side of the ship. He held out his hand for help but his countrymen standing by did nothing. A girl was whipped out of a canoe by one – the first case I have heard of.

I have enclosed some letters for you – one Report of the Kew Gardens I thought not worth sending, as you will visit Kew and can look at one there. I don't wonder at your mother being anxious about you. I shall answer her note soon. Oswell[44] is home from school and in Hamilton. Cannot see except by holding the book far off – Thomas with bloody urine – fever every evening – sweats – great thirst – was ordered by Dr Buchanan to have wine but it caused palpitations. It seems like our fever, does it not?

Ever yours with affection
David Livingstone

23

Tavistock Hotel
Covent Garden
London W.C.
July 28th, 1864

My Dear Dr Kirk,

A note with the photographs you kindly sent was the third I have been favoured with since I came home. I could not write before this but expected to be North instead, where I hope to see you. I am in a whirl at present but hope to break off at a tangent. I might have sold the *Lady Nyassa* at Bombay but could not bring my mind to give up Africa, so took a run home to consult. I would have gone up the Juba as we came but had only Pennell, Collyer and John Reid – with seven Zambesians, quite raw fellows. Rae left at Zanzibar to make his fortune by sugar. He was terrified lest we should go to Ras Dafoon and tried to infuse equal terror into the crew. The Resident at Aden shewed me a thousand dollar bond, signed by Macmillan and Rae, to the Arab who saved them and never was a penny paid!

I have seen Meller who I am sorry to say was very poorly and thin. Rowley took off a boy. M.[45] had baptised him much to Meller's disgust. Waller is in high glee at having got the better of Bishop Tozer in the affair of the boys. I am glad you were at the Geographical when Cooley[46] delivered himself. You hit the nail on the head. I am to be at Bath. I had an opportunity of speaking to Lord Palmerston.[47] He takes great interest in our work and so does Lady Palmerston. Indeed they are the great agents in what is done to put down slaving. It has been his life's work and aim to promote freedom and human happiness. Lord Russell is very cold in his manner but Layard is a brick and I shall have an opportunity of obeying the latter's voice and telling him everything, as I am to dine there tomorrow evening. Between ourselves, it is to let matters be known in the proper quarter that keeps me here. My heart is rather sore – that bad boy[48] has got into the American Army and will be made manure of, for those bloody fields. Sorry to hear of Dr Millar's departure. I must get something done for Thomas. I never saw a congestion of the Kidney, except in fever. His aunt says that during the attack of the measles, he passed frightful quantities of blood as if mixed with soot – I suppose she means per urethra. Can you come over to Young's at Limefield when I come. We could talk over matters there. Is your mother well – please present my compts. I met a school fellow [of] yours, a missionary at Poonah in India. You will excuse shortness, as I am very busy and worried.

Ever yours
Affectionately
David Livingstone

I met Sewell[49] the other day, going out to Borneo under Miss Coutts'[50] auspices!

24

Hamilton
September 1st, 1864

My Dear Dr Kirk,

I am glad to hear that you are enjoying yourself famously.
I too had a turn in the Highlands by Staffa and Iona and
Ulva and Mull. The weather was delightful and my native
air quite set me up again. I got a free passage and a ticket,
'at any time to and from any place'. See what it is to come
from rich ancestors! My ancestral Hall presents walls only,
which have never been high and the corn patches were small,
but I was glad I saw it. I had a very delightful trip and today
have sat down to my speech, the thought of which always
brings a cold shiver over me. I shall say that you will be
there and hold forth on the botany and natural history
– shall I?

I intended to have gone into Syme's hands ere now but
don't like to get my infirmities put into the News papers.
The bleeding has stopped and I feel very well. Syme said
that he believed it was a mistake to think the haemorrhoids
relieved the portal system. I know it relieved headache in
me often. Thomas is much better and at Youngs. I am
going to Bath of course – worse luck. The Portuguese Du-
pratt and Lavradio have been at Waller, pumping him as to
whether I shall be at Bath. Waller says now for shot grape
and cannister. Rowley wanted Wikatani and Chuma[51] home
from Bombay, to lionize with them.

Ever etc
David Livingstone

NEWSTEAD ABBEY
1864 : 1865

25

Newstead Abbey
Mansfield, Notts.
October 17th, 1864

My Dear Dr Kirk,

I have got a form of application all ready for your salary for three or four years and I think it will be effectual but on looking again at your last letter, I see it is left in doubt whether that would be agreeable or not. You simply say you would not like an unpaid job.

I dont wish to be troublesome but should feel obliged if you kindly say whether you would like the Expedition salary and the work as proposed in Dr Hooker's letter. When I get your reply I shall proceed with my application to Lord Russell.

Hoping this may find you at Edinburgh.

I am etc
David Livingstone

26

Newstead Abbey
Mansfield, Notts.
October 21st, 1864

My Dear Kirk,

I am very sorry to hear your determination not to engage in the proposed work, for I am quite sure that you would give information to the world of great value – and besides making your name better known, you would be in a fair way of getting something better. You will excuse me if I urge you to reconsider the subject. I am purposely avoiding anything like scientific description, having said in the introduction that it is hoped that you will give the botany and natural history of the Expedition (in the way that Darwin did of the *Beagle's* voyage). I mention sometimes that certain beasts were seen or killed and always when possible use *we*, referring to you and myself as Dr L. and Dr K. and I would give you the proof sheets, that you might see if I encroached too much on your province – and give you any information I could on the habits of some of the animals – though I dare say you know more on that subject than I do. Your botanical knowledge is not elementary and I thought Welweitsch's was frightfully so. All the works on Natural history would be at your disposal, and by due acknowledgement you could work up most of the popular information they contain and the authors be thankful. You may see what can be done, though not in an open, above board line as yours would be, by Routlege's *Natural History*, I think he calls it. You had better think over the matter again and if you change your mind please let me know. You might consult Dr Smith with advantage and to him and Lady Smith, you will kindly remember me.

[David Livingstone]

27

Newstead Abbey
Mansfield, Notts.
November 3rd, 1864

My Dear Kirk,

I delivered your message this morning and was blamed for not putting it strong enough to you. Mrs W. [52] says you can do your mammalia here – the heads in the Hall will inspire you and I am to say that you will have the room over mine and everything you want. It was not for a day or two I was to ask you but for a fortnight or three weeks. Her husband added 'and we may hear of something here as readily as they can do in London'. He thinks better of Nottingham than Cheltenham but I am to put it strongly, so you will consider this strong Kakamwe base. They are very nice people and seriously, I think it will be quite worth your while to make their acquaintance, both for their friendship at present and in the future. My brother[53] plus Yankee wife are invited to save me the trouble of going down to Scotland. He enjoys everything African. He is much troubled with one or two bits of cartilage floating about in his knee joint. I have objected strongly to any operation being attempted.

David Livingstone

28

Newstead Abbey
Mansfield, Notts.
November 7th, 1864

My Dear Dr Kirk,
I received your note and enclosures last week with many thanks, but fear that nothing can now be done to the rascally form that entrapped the poor fellow. I am glad to receive the admission of the Portuguese and put it in a footnote below what I have said of the inner channel having been used by slavers.
May I ask you what you intend to go in for. If for any situation, I would consider it a favour if you would call upon me to testify to your abilities etc. My recommendation might do you no harm and it would delight me if it could do you any good.
What is the name of the stinking plant we so often en-

*Group at Newstead Abbey—Chuma, Rev. Horace Waller, Susi,
Agnes Livingstone, Mrs Webb (seated), W. F. Webb and Tom Livingstone.
Photograph taken after Livingstone's death.*

countered? and is it the *Dolichos pruriens*, that cowitch stuff.
The people eat the bean very extensively farther North during the famine. I might mention the name of the plant that
gave you a headache, though all that sort of thing I have
already left out. Is the palmyra palm (*Palmyra brava*) properly called the Borassus Palm – and is the other called Hy-
phoene palm. I didnt think of naming them except in a
general way. Now that I am asking questions, might the
information you have given in the *Linnaean Transactions* be
used by me as notes or otherwise, due acknowledgement
being in every instance made. It would bring them into
notice and I should only take what is popular of them. I
have not seen anything of them but knowing whatever you
have written will be genuine I should like to use it, but not
without your sanction.

I shall be up at the meeting of the R.G.S. [54] on the 14th,
I hope.

David Livingstone

29

Newstead Abbey
Mansfield, Notts.
November 24th, 1864

My Dear Kirk,
I enclose two notes which will explain themselves. What
we have to do is to get the earliest information of any
vacancy which may take place. All feel that you deserve
something and I have no doubt but it will be secured. Are
the clubs places likely to afford the information required?
Are you acquainted with any one in the Colonial or Foreign
Office? I don't know anyone likely to be of service in the
first step of getting early information. The Hookers might.
Some of your friends might give you a hint in this for I am
quite at a loss.
    The Webbs – very nice people – want you down here for
a few days. He is president of some Mechanics Institute or
other at Mansfield and wishes me to say a little to help him
out with an hour's meeting. I said that you could do the
thing well and they both beg me to ask you. It would be
worth your while if not otherwise engaged – and also to
make the acquaintance of Lord Kinnaird[55] who with Lady
K. are really very good people. He has a great deal of influence with Lord Palmerston. Thanks for papers sent.
Sclater sends the others and I answer him about the Nakong.
If you decide to come, let me know as a carriage has to be

sent to the station, which is a private one. C. L's[56] wife is coming to England next mail.

David Livingstone

Will you give Arrowsmith[57] any sketches you have for the map?

30

Newstead Abbey
Mansfield, Notts.
November 25th, 1864

My Dear Kirk,
    Ask Arrowsmith for a letter I sent you yesterday, from
not knowing your address. It occurs to me just now you
ought to try to get information about appointments in the
East Indies. We may not get all we ask, but we shall get
more if we ask much than if aimed only at a little. All
readily admit that you ought to get something and should
a good thing turn up in India, I could try and get double
influence by asking Lord Russell or some other one to give
a note to Sir Charles Wood. [58] I would not cast myself away
in Kaffraria. The other letter contains an invitation here,
which you will answer to me at your convenience.
    I thought of a situation for Tom in an Indian Tea Com-
pany but he is poorly again. I ought to have taken him to
London with me but it escaped my memory and now he is
in Hamilton. Would you mind speaking to Dr Watson
about his case – which I stupidly neglected.
    The invitation here is thoroughly hearty from both Mr
and Mrs Webb.

David Livingstone

31

[Newstead Abbey]
November 27th, 1864

My Dear Kirk,

I put a question or two down just as I thought of them. I thank you for the compliment you pay to my name. If you can come, you need not be afraid of the meeting. Webb will say a little – you too, if there, on anything African and I conclude. That is all. Webb thinks York a good place for the like of you, as there is no good medico there and that you ought not to be thrown away.

What tree is it with which the bitter bark corn safes are made by the Badéma (Bandia's people). What is the name of the Sensi – the little animal they used to burn out of the islands?

Could you make an errand to the Colonial Office, to find out Col. Rigby's[59] despatch anent Roscher's discovery. I think I asked you before – but I fear he would communicate with India or the Indian Office. Captain Oldfield cannot charge his memory as to whether he received his information from Roscher or secondhand. I have set Agnes to look up the original letter of Oldfield to me.

Before you come down, will you give Murray's artist a loan of the photograph of the Baobab, the grave and Shupanga house to form with the fig tree one picture. I have only the Baobab and grave here.

I think Oswell only saw the Poku and it was not shot till afterwards. I think it is a Kobus but don't recollect distinctly. It is half brother to the Lechwe – a thorough water buck. Dr Gray (costume delle) has made Reade's striped Eland *oreas Derbyana* – Reade says it is called *Djikijunka* – a nice name. I saw Hartebeasts West of the Lake, a little less in size than [in the] south.

[David Livingstone]

32

Newstead Abbey
Mansfield, Notts.
December 1st, 1864

My Dear Kirk,

The little antelope called the Kualata is the bastard genisbuck of the Cape folk – and is figured in Harris as *aigoceros equina* or Roan Antelope. He has coloured it badly. It is called *Tagetse* by the Bechuanas, by the Makololo, *Kualata etsetta* or yellow *Kualata*. Harris' black buck is called by them *Potokuani* or *Kualata cencu*, black *Kualata* – they are so like, save the colour they are right I think.

The blue buck is a little thing and [its] skin is common as a bag. The Makololo call it *Gakitenoe* or *Hakitenove*. I am not 'stawed' scottice or scunnered from its goodness of flesh. I think, from what Webb tells me of the *Ourebi* in Natal, that the *Tianyawe* is no other than it.

Thanks for your attentions in going to Murray. I take it for granted you are coming, so you will be good enough on your way to take the enclosed fiddle to him for a wood cut and draw a handle to it. The string was a broad palm leaf, you remember – and say that the enlargement of the birds eye view, I am informed by Mr Bates, is at his service if he sends a properly accredited person for it. Baines has left out a distinct ravine parallel with the first and filled with trees, as you will remember.

Hoping to see you soon
I am etc
David Livingstone

Newstead Abbey
Mansfield, Notts.
December 8th, 1864

My Dear Kirk,

Many thanks for the papers you sent me yesterday and for the trouble you took in other matters.

I told Mr and Mrs W. how you are situated and I am requested to try and secure you for the 28th or 29th or say immediately after Christmas – can you be secured? It is for that meeting, I believe, as he is president but as Waller would say it is 'really and truly to know you besides and they are uncommonly nice people'.

C. L. comes on Monday and goes off in a day or two. He and his wife come here to save me a journey which otherwise I should have to make – as I never saw her. Waller is talked off his legs at Cambridge he says, and is to give a lecture at Croydon next week. He walks into Tozer and then says quite innocently 'they say very strong things about Tozer here'.

Have you seen Duke of Argyle's speech *contra* Darwin – it is good but wordy – I have written Rigby care of Colonial Office, but hear he is gone to India and today will address him there. Agnes[60] has looked through all my letters and can't find Oldfield's letter about the dates.

I am etc
David Livingstone

34

Newstead Abbey
Mansfield, Notts.
December 12th, 1864

My Dear Kirk,

You are to come at any time before the 28th or 29th that you like and stay a month if you can – for I was asked if you could not come before the time I mentioned and as I could not answer I was told to say as above. I hear the shooting going on just now.

I enclose a cheque for £10, which you will be good enough to bring in gold when you come. Say to the cashier that I had this cheque book with me in Africa and don't know if any alteration is required as to stamps.

Bring please a black doll, dressed, for one of the little girls, for 4 or 5 shillings (and pay yourself out of £10). One has a black doll and I wish to give one to the other. Admiral Sir George Lambert is here and so is Lord David Kennedy, a great Indian hunter, but very modest civil fellow – and if you don't mind burdening yourself, buy a couple of Shetland woollen drawers – the Shetland shop nearly opposite the School of Geology, Jermyn St. – white, soft thick woollen is the kind. Are you up in fish culture. We are going to try it here with the trout. What is the jumping fish. Is it a Goby? Send a line to say on what particular day and by what train at King's Cross you come.

David Livingstone

35

Newstead Abbey
Mansfield, Notts.
December 19th, 1864

My Dear Kirk,

Will you oblige me by bringing a bottle of Hair stuff. I found one kind called 'Molena' good but any kind will do. I bathe all over every morning and the hair becomes very dry after it. I asked Waller to put you to that trouble and my object in writing is to request you to bring a yard or so of Magnesium wire. Mrs Webb was expressing a wish just now that she could see it burning and I said that I would ask you to bring a little. She said to tell him 'that he is expected'.

Excuse my troubling you so.

David Livingstone

Is Jumping Johnny not a *Blennius*. The habits correspond better than with the Goby, only he has a little crest, but don't trouble yourself to write. The Banana seeds are now on their way down here. My brother searched my boxes in London for them on Saturday.

36

Newstead Abbey
Mansfield, Notts.
February 11th, 1865

My Dear Kirk,

I heard from Captain Chapman yesterday that Sunley[61] has not given up the consulate, but still I think that as no consul overlooks Mosambique, it would be well to set it before the Government. As Sir Roderic[62] likes to do a good turn, I shall write to him today to that effect.

Chapman thinks that Fraser[63] has given Rae a high offer and got him. He would then take sulks and leave Sunley. Chapman thinks badly of the affair.

I have seen the paper in *Good Words* since receiving your note this morning, though I had it by me some time previously. It is about what one would expect.

The microscope had arrived safely and I gave your address which had been previously asked for. A little more power might have been better but I suppose that could not have been secured for the money. I write to Dr Buchanan today. Tom will go to Arrowsmith's when it is a little milder. The fish are getting on – but slowly.

I am etc
David Livingstone

37

Newstead Abbey
February 13th, 1865

My Dear Kirk,

I am overcrowding you with letters, but a week ago a box turned up in charge of the Rev^d. C. A. Alington[64] which he found without address at the Cape. It contains specimens in bottles, he says – and thinks it may be Thornton's but I think it more likely to be yours as Young had especial charge of all Thornton's and reported them safe at Portsmouth long ago. I thought it best to direct Alington to send it with a note to Dr Hooker to Kew, where it would be identified. I explained to him why I thought it yours and asked if any others were left at the Cape – but have had no reply as yet. Will you take the trouble to examine it?

Would it not be well to speak to Lord Dalhousie about using his influence with Lord Russell for the Consulate. It would keep you before his mind if anything turned up. I stated particularly to Sir R. 'with sufficient salary'. It is necessary to hold that up, for they might offer a vice [Consulship] which is worth nothing. If however the vice C. meant £500, it would be a step to Tananarivo. The Webbs would use all their influence if anything could be heard of and be glad to do it.

He is beginning to think that the ova had too little milt because they don't come out.

D. Livingstone

38

Newstead Abbey
February 14th, 1865

My Dear Kirk,

Dr Peters[65] might as well come down gracefully and to
help him, you might say that on employing a native, whose
language I knew as well as any Portuguese knows the dialects
of Tette, to enquire the name of a mountain, he replied 'they
call it *Kaia* or as Dr Peters spells it *Caiia*' – and I put that
down as the name of the mountain referred to. It is no dis-
grace for a man to make a mistake of the kind. Mr Moffat[66]
has been collecting words in the Sechuana language for the
last 43 years – and finds new ones every week. In eight years,
I had upwards of seven thousand and I rejected many hun-
dreds either as uncouth or to me quite useless. Who but a
mad philologist would collect at least a score for the different gaits or modes of walking as erect, stooping, leaning
backwards, sideways, from side to side, wriggling, lifting
the feet high, very straight, slouching, swaggering. I think
there were eleven names for a lion and no end of words
meaning different shades of fools. Dr Peters' vocabularies
are wonderful on account of their gross inaccuracies and the
ability displayed by Dr Bleek in making so good a use of
such a jumble as they contain. There is scarcely a page but
contains as gross mistakes as this and one sees the mistakes
are made by the Portuguese element employed. The Dr
makes a bad shot with *pēnu*, seeing it is never pronounced
painoo – and does not mean (except inferentially) 'I don't

know'. The *e* is the same as in our word *hen*, as the word is used as we do the words *perhaps, it may be, possibly, is this the way*, or *is this right. Penu* – perhaps it is – inferentially of course it is *I don't know.* The majority of Tette fowls live in the huts of the people and not on perches. I cannot recollect two *aā's* in any native word, but *penu*, they may exist.

You will see whether it has been a misprint by consulting Bleek's book.

Mr Webb gave me yours to answer about the words – and you may quote me if you like.

I remember the hill very well. I say – a conical hill from which a large piece had peeled off granitic fashion like a por-tion of the flake of an onion – but I don't know the proper word for flake.

Mosambique wont do but Bambatook Bay would, I think – and as soon as I hear from Sir Roderick will write to Lord Russell and make use of Col. Playfair's[67] absence as an argument. I think you had better write to Dalhousie[68] too.

Thanks for your thoughts about Tom. I send Dr Lou-den's letter and write a note today to Dr Watson.

[David Livingstone]

39

[Newstead Abbey]
February 24th, 1865

My Dear Kirk,

I enclose a note from Prof. Buchanan about Tom, though it does not contain much. It is an answer to my request.

The fish are wagging their tails now in this thaw. We can see them distinctly moving and one empty shell has been found.

D. L.

40

Newstead Abbey
February 28th, 1865

My Dear Kirk,

I return you the paper on the dye stuff with many thanks, and also for the trouble you have taken about Tom. I shall thank Dr Watson by and bye. If you could give a proof of your papers to Mr Murray[69] when you have corrected it, time would be saved, and at the top put 'From the Transactions of etc.' of the date of its publication. I suppose no one would take offence – but this you will be best judge of.

I don't believe that the Government would take any part of the Sultan of Zanzibar's dominions, in as much as it would give the Tories a hold on them for taking new territory while unable to manage what they already have. Lord Stanley[70] and all his party would do anything for power – and all the nonsense he talked meant only 'let us change sides'. His father did a great deal he would now fain undo. It is a pity that Pine is such a fool, though a clever writer. Burton's weakness is notoriety. He would do anything for that. His saying that the Mahometans alone made converts on the West Coast, was meant only to shock and make people talk – seeing, except when they conquer, Mahometans never make headway.

We got a large number of eggs yesterday from Mr Hall's

Zanzibar, from the roof of the British Agency, July 1884.
Photograph by Kirk.

pond. He shifted 1,000 trout from one pond to another and we brought over two bait pans *full*. The fish is full formed in the billiard room and wags his tail.

I am, etc
David Livingstone

41

Newstead Abbey
Mansfield, Notts.
March 5th, 1865

My Dear Kirk,

I intend to come to London on Saturday next. Mr Layard wishes to say something to me on my own affairs. I don't know what, and it will be a good opportunity to talk to him about you. If I can get at Lord Russell, naturally I shall do the same to him.

Sir Roderick tells me that on 13th a meeting is to be held on Dessication of Southern Africa. I suppose you will be there. I mean to point out Nyanja, i.e. Motope or Nyanja pangono, which will delight the Portuguese. Will you do it if I speak of the other parts. You must have noticed that the Nyanja, i.e. Motope or pangono, was once a Lake, by the marks on the hills, and so was Nyanja Mokulu or *mucuru* (Elephant marsh). Remember how that fool Dafandata led

us round the hills towards the marsh when we were innocently asking for Nyanja Mokulu as if that were Nyassa till
Masakasa was going to throw him into the grass. I think
you might make a speech on it and it is well to keep yourself
before the public.

Noanje grows wild if I mistake not – and two wild grasses
besides are used as food. Do you remember the names of
them. I mean to mention them in connection with the sav-
age state. I sent off your sheet the same day I got it – came
back and suspecting the postman gone, sent for him, and
the Butler took some others and left yours in the box. I saw
it next day, but I hope it did not put you to inconvenience.
I am glad to hear of Tom.

I am, etc
David Livingstone

42

Newstead Abbey
Mansfield, Notts.
March 21st, 1865

My Dear Kirk,

Has any action taken place in consequence of my repre-
sentation to Mr Wild? He said that he would state what I
said to Lord Russell. I forgot to mention, I think, that he
said the whole of our affairs both in the East and West must
be revised. We must have some one to fill Baikie's place.
We cannot allow all he has done to be lost. A company
wants a subsidy and I think it must be granted etc etc, but
Mr Hammond[71] is the great advocate in the F.O. for
stinginess.

Do you remember how many promontories exist on the
N.E. side below or beyond the falls. My recollection is
that I went on the first till I found it too narrow and then
went, after getting my book, on after you and C. to the
second. Then there was a third or fourth which Baines does
not give, filled with trees at bottom and no water. I should
like to know if your recollections are the same as mine. Mr
Webb is going to Buxton for shampooing, the knee being
still locked. He says that would be a good place for you
but I dont know.

David Livingstone

Again in haste for the post.

43

Newstead Abbey
Mansfield, Notts.
March 24th, 1865

My Dear Kirk,

I feel very much annoyed at the refusal to print your reply. They ought to have refused Peters too, but this knuckling down to the Germans shews them to be no great things themselves. There is an immense deal of 'claw me and I'll claw you' in the bowing to the Germans' immaculate conceptions. I have fired a shot at the thing *Kaia*[72] but had a 'grave Berlin Professor' till last revise and I put out Berlin. I enclose a proof that you may see.

Dry cupping has been tried, it has made the skin looser and I think, straightened the leg but it is still to a certain degree locked. In speaking tonight, they both urged that you should press Lord Dalhousie now that Parliament is going to be dissolved, to ask for a Consulate – a definite promise in black and white. They will do anything for an influential man like him. It is only by pressing that anything can be got. You know him, I suppose. If you think that it would do any good, give me his address and I could write him at the same time or send my letter to you, if you think a reference to me would help. The way my brother got his was not through me except indirectly (and I am to get no salary) and so that I would not be blate to apply for another. I think that really it is high time that pressure should be applied for it is evident to me, Mr Wild having spoken to Sir Roderick, that after he had reported what I said to Lord Russell, His Lordship must have said 'see what Sir Roderick says first'. Suppose you put the case fairly to Lord Dalhousie – no consulate on the whole 900 miles of coast which the Portuguese claim nor on an equal line of Madagascar, where slaving is going on, etc., etc.' The Comoro consulate being a mere nothing and the Zanzibar one having too much to do – then no scientific results to be expected, besides the consulate having by a vote of the Lords being insisted on; but at Bambatouk-bay this would be accomplished without the Government being forced to follow the vote, etc. Anything that will make a good case, if fairly in Lord Dalhousie's head, would I feel sure help you, and so many people approach that unless pressure is put on nothing will be done.

I am etc
David Livingstone

44

Newstead Abbey
Mansfield, Notts.
March 27th, 1865

My Dear Kirk,

What do you call the tree from which the bark cloth is made? – and the Molompi – would it be sufficient to say a *Ptero carpus* – the *vallis nerid*? for the Lake plant of which they make salt and is the *Sarsaparilla* of the hills known. It was the Mosibe that was previously known in the West Indies and nowhere else, was it not – the seed with a red pellicle which was fattening. The Mboma or Boma is also oil yielding, I think – what do you call the Fustic? I did not put anything of that kind down because I expected that the Government would have employed you to describe them all.

Mr Webb's knee is a little better but still locked, he goes about today for [the] first time. I think the thing must be in a dent in the cartilage. The fish are dying just coming out. It is far too cold for them to hatch out.

I am etc
David Livingstone

In one note you say *Aula-clodus swinderianus*, in another *Aulacodus swindernianus*.

28th. I am glad that your reply is to be printed, and think

you were quite right to object to the Speke scheme. I was written to about three months ago to attend that meeting and it would, they said, be put off till it was convenient – I let them know that it never would be convenient – the slave trade must be suppressed as the first great step to any mission – that baffles every good effort. I see Lord Stanley is in the hands of the oil traders again. The native Christians in Sierra Leone contribute £10,000 annually to the Church Mission.[73]

45

[Newstead Abbey]
March 28th, 1865

Private

The cartilage that has been locking the joint came out this morning and Mr and Mrs Webb go off to London for advice to Fergusson and perhaps Paget. We put a ring round the cartilage and a pad over the spot from which it appeared to have come out, and they are off. I promised Mrs W. to write a private note to you and she will let you know when they are settled, as she would have much more confidence in the opinion of a friend than of others. You will please object quite strongly against any operation till the path of the thing out of the joint is obliterated. You will thereby do a kindness to Mrs W. I said keep the thing where it is and press it down till in its own sack and then *operate* and I hinted that he had better ask the surgeons to guarantee him a supple and not a stiff joint if they operate now. They will be at 51 Upper Brook Street, but I gave her your address.

David Livingstone

46

Newstead Abbey
Mansfield, Notts.
April 5th, 1865

My Dear Kirk,

I have written to Lord Dalhousie today and put the thing to him pretty fairly. I brought you to his recollection by his kindness to your Father, and told him all about the West Coast of Madagascar and Zanzibar, and begged his influence with Lord Russell and Sir Charles Wood and I think he wont be offended from the way I put the whole matter.

They called the stuff Mukuru where I got it.

If necessary I could write to Sir Bartle Frere, a first rate man, Governor of Bombay, but if Lord Dalhousie speaks to Sir C. Wood it will be better.

I got a letter from Mr Moffat yesterday. Sekeletu died of the disease last February or March, after sending to Mr

Moffat asking him to write and thank me for a couple of horses and £50 of goods I sent by way of Kuruman.

Manūre and Mamodusane have been fighting for the regency and Manūre, beat, fled to Lake N'gami and returned with the people there to steal the Makololo cattle. So as seems likely things there are in a mess. Where does Welweitsch hold forth? The *London Advertizer* was 'much exercised' on my orthodoxy, a Scotch paper says, after bishop Colenzo[74] drank my health – and accused me of ingratitude to the London Missionary Society[75] because, having received some theological training – he says 'all my education' – I do not continue its slave for ever!

David Livingstone

47

Newstead Abbey
Mansfield, Notts.
April 14th, 1865

My Dear Kirk,
You will see by the enclosure that Lord Dalhousie is all right and in your favour. Lord Russell will see by my letter to the Earl that I *think* a good deal, like the Cabby, though I says little. It would be well if possible to get some positive information as to *Col.* Playfair's[76] intentions, something tangible, if the West Coast of Madagascar, the advantages of which as overlooking Mosambique I pointed out, should be refused. It is rather a joke between ourselves my urging your claims as infinitely above Mellers, the said Meller being Lord Russell's own protege.

If anything tangible could be urged on Sir C. Wood it would prevail. Don't mention my not getting any salary nor anything else – we may prevail yet.

Thank you for the opinion about the 'Millukuru'. It must be from a tree and from the account I got of it I suspect it was used with 'Ufa' to make it go over greater surface on their heads.

I am etc
David Livingstone

48

[Newstead Abbey]
April 30th, 1865

My Dear Kirk,

By a note from Waller I learn that Meller has got a commission and a roving one too to Madagascar, and a good salary – and I can't but feel sorry that your claims have not been pressed on the Foreign Office, as this lessens your chance there. I have no doubt but Lord Dalhousie would do you a good turn if you put it fairly before him and so many apply that one who does not press himself forward has but little chance. One should not be sorry at the success of another, but this somehow makes me very sorry, for I am sure you would have done the duties and advanced scientific and moral interests a thousand times better than our friend Meller, but I suppose it has been through Lady Russell that his claims have been advanced. Do let me urge, even to the extent of boring you, to try Lord Dalhousie. Meller will be for the interior, I suspect, and the West Coast, as overlooking Mosambique, has claims of its own and if you will try and at the same time give me his Lordship's address, I would presume to write to him too.

Many thanks for the note about the Mosibe. I enclose a red powder they use on their heads West of Nyassa, whether of vegetable or earthy origin I could not ascertain.

Gunner Young has made a wail to Captain Wilson against

me for not getting him storage money. I certified twice to the Admiralty that he had kept the stores. This was sufficient for George and May. Then to save him any trouble in case of my death, [I] left a paper in his charge when I went last up to the Lake, certifying do., do., and recommending him for promotion to Admiral Walker and Washington. The Admiralty wouldn't give him what he wanted and expected, and Wilson, believing all that Young says about it, blames me. He might as well blame the Admiralty, though I suppose that is rather a stale subject for blame.

I am etc
David Livingstone

It is very pretty and like carmine. Will you say what it is ?[77]

49

8 Dover Street
London
May 13th, 1865

My Dear Kirk,

Agnes wont undertake the selection of a vignette, so I must do the best I can. You remember a sphax which used to kill tsetse, a long bodied rakish craft of an insect. I don't know its native name but Oswell called today and he thought of it. I shall take the scroll to Murray on Monday morning and see what he thinks. I set Waller to draw a man in a slave stick and the slave trader holding the end [*pen drawing in text*] with a gun in his hand. The sawing would be better. See if you can't light on something better – We have a bird's eye view of the falls as a Frontispiece – from one I sent home in 1860. Palms however are home manufacture. It gives a good idea of them.

Waller called with Alington yesterday. The latter would like to go with me and I believe pay his own expenses, as he did with the Mission. He is a good fellow – knows a little Zulu from going into Panda's country. I told him what we have for the whole thing – £500 from F.O., £500 from R. G. S. and £1,000 from a private friend. I would rather go alone than take anyone untried. I suffered too much from Bedingfeld & Co. I would be delighted if we could be together but I fear the money wont reach a salary. Could Lord

Dalhousie not manage a salary for you – I mean to go up Rovuma to where we turned in boats – make Ndonde's a depot for goods – not many for I don't mean to waste them as Speke and Burton did, nor go in grande array – twenty or twenty five Indians. Sir Bartle Frere told [me] that they were very reliable and faithful – I would not bring them into contact with Zanzibarites at all. Then go up along Rovuma westwards of whom we heard as good and having many buffaloes in their country. Then get into communication with the Mazitu, if they are still further west – and if they are to the south go among the Manganja who are great elephant hunters about Bemba and work quietly west.

We were always in too great a hurry last expedition. I would have more time and get better acquainted with the natives and try to give them some idea of our objects as we go along.

I told Alington that I would take tea, coffee and flour to last a long time but not much else – and that he might think about it.

What do you say to a talk with Lord Dalhousie about it? I shall be here till 23rd.

Thanks for the information about poor Baikie. It is very sad. I did not quite believe May's stories. Of course I shall keep it secret but it does appear sad, and enough to discourage the F.O. altogether.

Rowley talked two hours yesterday. Waller called the Anthropologists Icebergs, floating down the warm stream of humanity, chilling all who came near them.

Agnes sends her kind regards and thanks for the offer of a ticket, and so do I to your mother, hoping she is better.

I am etc
David Livingstone

50

Burnbank Road
Hamilton
June 8th, 1865

My Dear Kirk,

I took a run over to Young's a week ago and thence went to Edinburgh to talk to Lord Dalhousie but was unfortunate enough to find him at the Assembly on the last day of meeting. When that was over I was too fatigued with gadding about to feel that I could appear to advantage and it was too late for a call besides. I had to come away here for I had promised to come back, my mother being very far gone, I fear sinking gradually – and not long for this world. She had Bronchitis. The lower part of the lungs seems to be impervious – and she feels as if she is choking. At her age, 82, no hope of recovery can be entertained. I have got Stewart to make enquiries as to Lord Dalhousie's whereabouts without saying what my object is, and if I can leave my poor mother, will make a journey to where he may be.

I was just an afternoon and a morning at Young's, and did not see your brother or the new works.

I have written to Sunley for Johanna men. It does not seem feasible to go into Mombasa and hand oneself and goods over to people of whom we know next to nothing and on whom we have no hold. I may get a few of some other tribe of Indians from Sir Bartle Frere as a body guard.

He is a very able man without doubt and has worked himself up by sheer ability alone, so not withstanding anything
to the contrary, I think there will be no mistake in placing
some reliance on him.

Tom's complaint comes back if he over exerts himself,
which from feeling hearty and strong he is rather inclined
to do – or if he gets a cold. He has grown a great deal and is
growing fast. He got a prize for drawing yesterday – the picture was exhibited and is very much better than I had any
idea of. He must be taking after his father! who is great in
that line!! Oswell got prizes for being dux in six departments. Yesterday I went to see the distribution – German,
Geography, Scriptural knowledge, French and Latin, etc.
The recitations in German and English far exceeded anything I ever saw when I was a boy. We hear nothing of poor
Bob and I fear never will. I think that it cannot be denied
that the Confederates treated their prisoners cruelly. They
had not rations enough for their soldiers, and we cannot
wonder that they starved their prisoners. It would be a pity
if they hung Davis, but I cannot conceive why he is so
lauded as a high-minded gentleman. He fought that he and
others might be served without paying servants wages. We
don't call a man a gentleman who can't and wont pay his
way. The North has a gigantic task now in undoing all that
slavery has done in debasing these millions of negroes – of
course they wont work now, nor should I if I had been a
slave.

I got my evidence to correct but had already corrected it
in a copy of Mr Arthur Mills and trusted him to deliver it
but he has forgotten and it will go uncorrected with several
mistakes in it which I regret but I recommended the keeping up the settlements. The words 'strong native *princes*'!!
Do they mean to hold up fellows like Dahomey – Docemo,
King Peppel, etc. If so, that is a mistake. A strong middle

class of Christian traders should be formed and though not equal to a middle class elsewhere they would be prevented by each other from glaring wrongs. If I get to Edinburgh soon, I will call on your mother.

David Livingstone

51

Burnbank Road
Hamilton
June 24th, 1865

Dear Dr Kirk,

Our very sincere and deep sympathy with you in the sore loss, we see by today's paper, you have sustained. All the more cordial inasmuch as we have had the same tender ties severed ourselves. I wrote a note yesterday.

David Livingstone

52

Newstead Abbey
Mansfield, Notts.
July 30th, 1865

My Dear Kirk,

Webb's case seems entirely neuralgic. He walks about and does not seem ill except when the fits come on. I gave 10 drops of chlorodyne last night and have not seen him this morning but there is no cause for alarm – perhaps not for going to London – nor for anyone coming down unless he became worse. Oswell very gladly came with us and immersed in African and the rocky mountains legends he seemed to forget all about his complaints.

Baines demands that I should say that I dismissed him without a hearing and was led by the evidence of my brother alone. As that is not true, I shall not tell a lie. I myself saw that the goods were gone and asked him whither. He offered to pay for them and begged to be allowed to stay with us without salary – this was to myself. The other confession was simply a corroboration. I published nothing and endured all the abuse he himself published, in silence. If he publishes here while I am within hearing, I certainly will not be so forbearing. I did not wish to part with him and gave him a full opportunity of defending or explaining at Kongone. When he sneeringly denied that any loss had occurred, there was nothing for it but that he must go, unless I were to take the onus of the party suffering privations which might have been prejudicial to life, merely to screen a store-keeper from whose charge the goods had gone in some way which he best knew.

Tito told me himself that Baines had given him Expedition provisions but he added 'com minto medo a Senhor'. Why should he fear me if he were doing right? Sir Roderick shewed me a similar letter to that you have received. It demands that I withdraw as publicly as I made the charge. I published nothing and had he only held his tongue it would now have been forgotten.

Capt. Gardner wants your address. His is 43 Crescent, Clifton. He has given me a long extract from his letter book, shewing that the Portuguese declared that they had no power in Antonio River but he fears my publishing it. When punishment was demanded by the *Wasp* for an outrage on a boat's crew, the Governor General said he had no power but they carefully avoid giving a letter to that effect.

I am etc
David Livingstone

Mr and Mrs Webb's very kind regards.

INDIA

1865 : 1866

53

Poonah
September 20th, 1865

My Dear Kirk,
    We arrived at Bombay on the morning of the 11th and heard that the mail steamer, which had left a day before, contained Col. Playfair, said to be ill of heart disease and frequent fits of syncope – otherwise he does not look ill. Dr Seward is acting Political Agent in his absence. He has not resigned but I imagine he will not attempt to return. As it is I could not well say more about you to the Governor than what regarded your general fitness for that service. If Playfair resigns, I think his place would be filled up at home. Had he resigned here, it would likely be filled up here, for I was asked by a Political Officer whether the place were empty with a view, as I imagined to an application. It would be well now to get your claims pressed on Sir Charles Wood by Lord Dalhousie, so that in case of anything happening your claims might not be forgotten. I trust that you will lose no time about it. The Governor is very willing to do what he can for my next trip. I am at his house now and very kind he is in the way of aiding my arrangements for the future of my own work.
    Bombay is very hot just now but the air up here is cool and pleasant. The slopes of the Ghauts are splendid and covered with jungle and grass, which look very much like

some parts of African scenery. Many of the plants are to the eye in passing identical. Here mapiva and mexoeira are as common as in Africa but smaller. The Euphorbia round the villages of the Manganja is seen here in hedges and the thorny acacia with long white thorns is the common tree. Seventeen inches is the rainfall at Poonah, while 150 inches fall on the edge of the ghauts. All who can afford to leave Bombay now do so but Society consists chiefly of the military and their wives and balls and other like diversions are common. I walk as much about here as in Africa but all are so afraid of their heads that I adopt a big hat, not to be singular. It is not likely that I shall leave before November. I am to get some men of the Marine Battalion who have been accustomed to rough it and I am thinking of buffaloes as an experiment worth trying for the tsetse but I am not yet clear about it. I write only to urge you to try for Playfair's place. It would be a great benefit to me to have you on the coast, so it is not altogether unselfish.

Affectionately yours
David Livingstone

The Sultan of Zanzibar is coming over here about December in state. You would be the better of a knowledge of Arabic. If you see a fair prospect, it would be well to learn a little.

54

Bombay
November 15th, 1865

My Dear Kirk,

I wrote you as soon as I heard of Col. Playfair's illness and would have telegraphed but all messages go by Government officials and I did not know whether the place were vacant or not. I sent it to 2 Belgravia (lower) and now feel anxious to know if you have made any efforts with Lord Dalhousie and Sir Charles Wood. I told the Governor here how valuable you would be on the East coast but he was silent.

I hear nothing from you and now, just before the steamer starts for Suez, write a line to ask if you have got my first letter from Bombay. If not, its purport was to get you to make an effort at once. I heard from Waller of 16th October and he relates the sad end of poor Rae and that you had left London for the North but not a word about Playfair's place and successor. I am now in suspense and very uneasy because I dont hear from the Admiral about a passage. I have sent off the buffaloes and 3 calves, 11 are beasts of burden, and to try the tsetse and now am on thorns about the Admiral saying nothing.

Mr Layard . . . [78] for a passage and said that nothing else was required. If you are at the F.O., speak to Mr Wylde to telegraph if necessary. I dont like to go in a dhow, it would be *infra dig*, or I should go tomorrow. I shall write you a longer and more connected letter next time. I went up as far as Ahmedabad. It is facsimile of many parts of Africa we have seen – the plants identical – Mapira Meshoeira all the go – and it is called the 'garden of India' . . .[79]

I got one letter from you. I have 12 sepoys – marines of the old company – one havildar, and eight Africans. Good bye, the steamer goes in ten minutes.

[David Livingstone]

55

Bombay
December 2nd, 1865

My Dear Kirk,

Dr Birdwood, the curator of the Botanical Garden and Museum here, told me yesterday that he would recommend you to the Governor as a fit person to occupy his place. He was at College with you, but did not know you otherwise than by sight. As it is likely from what I said to the Governor that you may get an offer, I shall try to give you as clear an idea of the affair as possible. The salary is 500 Rupees a month, say £50, or £600 a year with a good house which as rents have risen enormously, is as much more. He is going to ask an advance of pay and believes it will be R.700 a month or £840. This is not so much as it looks like owing to the high price of living now in Bombay. A horse and phaeton with horse boy and servants would cost you in your free house 300 R. or £30 a month, so with your R. 500 to 700 you would have £20 and £40 over, say £240 or £480 to save yearly. The cost of horse and phaeton would be £150. The house is in the Botanic Garden and that is new. The Museum is only building – and is rather a fine building at the entrance to the Garden. You would direct the planting out and select plants and seeds and have men under you to do the work – the situation is flat, and during the monsoon patches of water lie adjacent. Dr Birdwood has been the chief hand in getting up the Gardens and looks on them with great affection and hence his anxiety to get a fit occupant while he retires, I believe for a time, on account of want of health and having been ten years out in Bombay. He suffers from fever and his stomach cannot bear quinine or arsenic. He is rather desponding as to his state of health. The Governor's band plays in the Gardens and people flock to hear it. As you are a ladykiller, you might be successful in the matrimonial line there. Fruit and vegetables you would have free. The medical profession does not stand high and you would have a fair share – in time probably a large one – of the practice. Dr Birdwood devotes his time more to literary pursuits than practice, hence I guess his duties do not occupy a large portion of his time. He is Hon. Sec. of the Bombay Asiatic Society and something else which bring honour and bother only. My impression is that if nothing better turns up yet and the offer comes, you might accept it as a step in the right direction. If employed, the Governor would provide for you elsewhere in the event of Birdwood resuming his duties. He gave his private physician, Dr Steadman, a good appointment as head of the Sir Janisettjee Jhejeebhoy hospital – and there are many Scotch men here – and they are clannish but all making money and eager to go home. The climate is not good but with care, one may enjoy good health. Whether you ought to take this when offered as a stepping stone to something else or decline it as likely to shelve you into Indian ways, I can't say. It is an important step in life and with more risk than at home. I would run the risk for a higher stake than usually offers at home, but you must decide and I trust that God will give you wisdom to act for the best.

It is rather premature in me to write so much about what His Excellency may or may not do. I think it likely he will be disposed to make you an offer. He is a very good man – is accused of being too soft – but it is in manner only. When I hear more, I shall let you have it. This goes by a new company started by Americans 'Stearns Hobart & Co.' who send cotton by the over-land route and charge £60 passage money from there to Liverpool. I am living with one of them Mr Stearns, a very good fellow. I don't know my starting day and hence I write now in case of being called off. All my men are ready. I am not to wait for a man of war but go in one of . . .[80] Osborne's fleet called *Thule*, a present to the Sultan of Zanzibar. Seward is acting there – no appointment has been made.

Affectionately yours
David Livingstone

A sad end was that of poor Rae. Mr Brown of the same company here says that they are disassociated from the Sultan now. They will hire their labour in the open market. He does not know of Rae's brother coming out. Is Rae's wife his heir?

56

Bombay
December 13th, 1865

My Dear Kirk,

In reference to my last, I find that Dr Birdwood can not say more, till he has seen the Governor and that will probably be between 15th and 20th curr^t. He complains of getting worse, so I think is not likely to stay long in this country – I gave you as fair an account as I could of the advantages and disadvantages of the situation (if offered). I would take it only as a stepping stone if nothing better offers – I think that the practice would in time surpass anything in a country town but I don't know much in that line. If the Governor invites you, I suppose he would do you a good turn, if opportunity offered afterwards, but this is merely conjecture.

I am in daily expectation of orders to embark on the *Thule* by which ship I am to go, but probably the Governor will come about 13th and give the necessary orders to sail. I am very tired of doing nothing.

The Africans who came with me have lost the peculiar odour and now emit the peculiar Indian mousey or Aloetic smell!! I have observed it ever since my return and they complain of weakness. The Arabs imbibe the African odour on the continent and you remember what we imbibed at Kongone.

Grant has been feasted at Calcutta – Scotchmen predominate there as well as here and all are pretty clannish. No news from the coast for a long time. The weather is now cool and pleasant here – but I wish I were away to my work.

Very affectionately yours
David Livingstone

57

Bombay
New Years Day, 1866

Private

Many happy returns of this day to you.

My Dear Kirk,

The Governor sent for me yesterday and from the contents of your letter which I received the day before I guessed the purpose. He said that he wished to ask me about you. He knew that I had always spoken very handsomely about you but there were sometimes private circumstances in a man's character, which unless called upon to reveal, no one would think of mentioning. There may be something (here I put in the word 'cranky'), yes something that though not prominent might render him an inconvenient public servant. I replied in terms that I need not repeat that I knew no defect of character, or temper. You got on well with people but were firm in doing your duty, etc. and I felt certain that, from your hatred to the slave trade and knowledge of the whole subject, you would be invaluable at Zanzibar. He said that it was a great recommendation that I wished you to be there and he would have much pleasure in telegraphing to you today and he wished me to write a letter to you to go by next mail. I do this now and as I am to go by tomorrow morning in the *Thule*, I can only congratulate you on your appointment.

I have spoken to Tracey to shew you kindness here – the hotels are horribly dear – and he will do his duty. He is big brother to Tracey of the *Orestes*. You should call on Michael Scott of the same firm with Tracey and a leading man here, now in London – and it would be well to see Fleming. Fraser is said to be out of his house now and Alexander Brown, the head of the Firm here and a very good fellow, tells me that they are to have nothing to do with the Arabs but to hire labour in the open market. I shall mention your coming to him – and to Mr Lidderdale, the head of Remington & Co., who is a great florist. The Scotch are clannish and will save you much expense. I have been thinking, if we could get an Arab settlement near [the] mouth of the Rovuma, positively free to all and without slavery, it might be a step in advance. It might be a way of establishing the Sultan's brother. Turn this over in your mind. He is here now (Poonah) and was operated on for *elephantiasis Scrotis* successfully and gave Dr Mackenzie a fine Damascus. . . .[81] Jan. 7th. The telegram went off yesterday. I thanked His Excellency and told him I had written to you. He is a real good fellow – is blamed for being too polite but is firm enough when necessary.

I go positively tomorrow.

[David Livingstone]

AFRICA
1867 : 1872

58

Msama's country
September 12th, 1867

I met Hamidi Mahamad in the Ulungu country and was very kindly treated by him and his brother headmen, Hamees Wodim Tagh and Syde bin Alli. Though they had suffered great losses in goods and men by a chief called Msama, they generously gave me cloth, beads and provisions and tried to make peace with Msama that they might pass through the country in search of ivory and that I might go where I chose. I was three and a half months with them, while negotiations were going on with Msama and believe they are totally different from the Kilwa traders on whose track we came up from the Rovuma to Nyassa and who fled from us invariably.

I give this to Hamidi Mahamad in acknowledgement of his good services and am etc

David Livingstone

59

My Dear Col. Playfair or Dr Kirk,

This note goes by Musa Kamaals[82], who was employed by Karoje to drive the buffaloes hither but by overdriving them unmercifully in the sun and tying them up to save trouble in herding, they all died before he got to Unyinyembe – he witnessed the plundering of my goods and got a share of them. I have given him beads and cloth sufficient to buy provisions for himself in the way back to Zanzibar. He has done nothing here. He neither went near the goods here nor tried to prevent them being stolen in the way – I suppose that pay for four months in coming, other four of rest, and four in going back, would be ample but I leave this to your decision. I could not employ him to carry my mail back nor can I say anything to him for he at once goes to the Ujijians and gives his own version of all he hears. He is untruthful and ill-conditioned and would hand off the mail to anyone who wished to destroy it.

The people here are like the Kilwa traders haters of the English. More Zanzibar men whom I met between this and Nyassa were gentlemen and traded with honour. Here, as in the haunts of the Kilwa hordes, slaving is a series of forays – and they dread exposure by my letters. No one will take charge of them. I have got Thani bin Suellim[83] to take a mail privately for transmission to Unyambe. It contains a cheque on Ritchie, Steuart & Co of Bombay for Rs 2,000 and some forty letters written during my slow recovery. I

Ujiji — 30th May 1869

My Dear Col. Playfair or Dr Kirk
This note goes by Musa
Kamaals who was employed
by Karoje to drive the buffaloes
hither, but by driving them unmercifully in the sun & tying them
up to save trouble in herding
they all died before he got to Unyanyembe — He witnessed the plundering of my goods & got a share of
them — I have given him beads
and cloth sufficient to buy provisions for himself in the way
back to Zanzibar — He has done
nothing here — He neither went
near the goods here nor tried to
prevent them being stolen in the
way — I suppose that pay for
four months in coming — other
four of rest — and four in going
back would be ample but
but I leave this to your decision
I could not employ him to
carry my mail back, nor can
I say anything to him for he
at once goes to the Ujijians

[left margin, vertical:] A long line might go on Ujiji was worth & say nothing of the price

Facsimile of part of letter on facing page.

fear it may never reach you. A party was sent to the coast two months ago. One man volunteered to take a letter secretly but his master warned them all not to do so
'because I might write something he did not like'.
He went out with the party and gave orders to the headman to destroy any letter he might detect in the way.

This, though I am good friends outwardly with them all. I can get no assistance in procuring carriers and as you will see, if the mail comes to hand, I sent to Zanzibar for fifteen good boatmen to act as carriers if required – 80 pieces of Merikans[84], 40 do Kinike, 12 Frasila's of the beads called Sam-sam, shoes etc and I have written to Seyed Majid,[85] begging two of his guard to see to the safety of the goods here into Thani bin Suellim's hands or into those of Muhamad bin Saleh.

As to the work to be done by me, it is only to connect the sources which I have discovered from 500 to 700 miles south of Speke and Baker's with their Nile. The volume of water which flows North from Lat. 12° South is . . .[86] as well as those of the Nile. I have to go down the Eastern line of drainage to Baker's turning point. Tanganyika-Nzige-Chowambi (Baker's?) are one water and the head of it is 300 miles south of this.

The western and central lines of drainage converge into an unvisited lake, West or S.W. of this. The outflow of this, whether to Congo or Nile, I have to ascertain. The people West of this, called Manyema, are cannibals if Arabs speak truly. I may have to go there first and down Tanganyika, if I come out uneaten and find my new squad from Zanzibar.

I earnestly hope that you will do what you can to help me with the goods and men. £400 to be sent by Mr Young must surely have come to you through Fleming. A long box paid for to Ujiji was left at Unyembe and so with other boxes.
David Livingstone

60

Private and Confidential   Bambarre
Manyema country
November 2nd, 1870

My Dear Col Playfair and Dr Kirk,

I shall give you in as few words as possible the state of my work and reserve a corner of this the last bit of paper I have here to notice anything I can, in the event of your long expected letters coming to hand.

This great lacustrine river Lualaba is the central line of drainage of the Great Nile Valley. It is, as you will have learned from letters in a large packet sent to the care of the Governor of Unyembe, Syde bin Salem Buraschid, in June 1869, first of all the Chambeze. This on emerging from the great Lake Bangweolo becomes the Luapula, and that on coming out of Lake Moero is Lualaba, at first eight or ten miles broad and then holding a width of from two to six miles and always deep as far as it is known. West of this, two large rivers, each having the same native name Lualaba, unite and form a Lake before going North into, I suppose, the Nile. Looking back from this Lake which I have by anticipation named Lake Lincoln, we have a remarkable mound on the Watershed from which four gushing fountains flow each to form a large river though at their sources not more than ten miles apart. Two on the North side form the two Lualabas mentioned, West of this, two on the

South side of the Zambesi. These are probably the 'unfathomable fountains of the Nile', mentioned to Herodotus by the secretary of Minerva in the city of Sais, from which 'half the water flowed Northward to Egypt, the other half to Inner Ethiopia'.

I have heard of this mound and its fountain so often at different distant points from the natives and from intelligent Arabs who have visited the spot that I cannot doubt more than if I had seen them myself. If I had men who had been taught to work, with my ordinary success, I could finish all the exploration in four or five months and then retire. My experience in Manyema has been trying – the vegetation is indescribably rank – the rills and rivulets innumerable and the mire or glaur grievous. When my attendants got fed and lodged at a camp, to which the rains compelled me to retire, by the slave women whose husbands were away collecting ivory, they refused my rations though a half more than those of the best fed slaves and went flaunting about in gaudy coloured lambas bought with the beads they now rejected. They pretended to fear a canoe when I was ready to go down Lualaba – I consented to refrain from buying one – they then feared the people though till advised by slaves, they are all remarkably friendly. The head Arabs spoke to them and they literally trembled and consented to go anywhere but when they found that no compulsion was to be used, refused duty again.

I went North with only three, my feet were torn by travelling in mire and instead of healing kindly as heretofore, an irritable eating ulcer fastened on each foot and laid me up for months – they are common here – a discharge of bloody itch with great pain each night may shew that they are allied to fever. Many slaves are killed by them. I was forced to come to a stand till men came from you and come back to Bambarre. If there had been bad blood as we say between my

people and me, I should not have been surprised at their taking advantage when I could get none of the Manyema to
carry, but I had a sore longing to finish my work and retire –
invited them three times over to take beads and food and
said, if they changed their minds, the goods were at their
service. When Muhamad Bogharib,[87] a good man, came,
they told him that I refused to give them beads! Their only
modern accomplishment is to lie without compunction. I
am unwilling to get into hot water with Revd. Simon Price,
the headmaster of Nassick School,[88] or with the bishop who
confirmed them all before leaving, but to send such Africans
forth as having been taught trades and being Christians is
little less than a public fraud. Mr Price could not have
known but the blacksmith confessed freely that he had
never welded iron, the carpenter could not cut a piece of
wood straight though I chalked it out for him, the mason
wanted his stones squared for him. They all believed that
when away from the Consul at Zanzibar, no punishment
could reach them – 'their teachers feared them and never
punished'. In this they had correctly judged for the masters
dreaded their desertion at Nassick and bringing an ill report
on the Institution. Whether you can do anything to them
for breaking their engagements with me and putting me to
enormous trouble, expense and loss of time, you will know
best. I send you a short statement I wrote some time ago – I
do not mention their eager slave hunting where no danger
existed for that happened since they deserted. It was annoy-
ing to see, as I did 'English subjects' marching in with captured women and children to ingratiate themselves with the
Arabs. The Manyema flee in terror at the reports of guns
and no danger is incurred in catching their children, wives
and goats. Abereme or Ibrahim went in spite of my orders
not to go, and captured two fowls and some tobacco! He
feared to go near till all the men and women had fled. Drice

is a yellow half-cast, Galla Muhamad Bogharib, bearer of this, is a good fellow. He has been unwearied in his kindness to me. He in fact saved my life – Pneumonia caught in Marungu.

Collecting ivory is like gold digging the tusks had been left in the interminable forests where the elephants had fallen – no trader came till now and the people, if civilly treated, bring them for a small price in copper bracelets. No trader can spare his people – a thousand dollars does not look half so large as the tusks each hopes to secure – hence having been laid up by ulcers for a long time, I thought it best to wait for men from you. If my packet of June 1869 was not destroyed, your men cannot be far distant. I sometimes fear its destruction, for a long box for which 15 dollars were paid to Palamotto to carry it to Ujiji was detained at Unyembe and not delivered, though I sent for it twice and goods to pay the carriers. It contains two guns and a pistol, medicines, letters etc. A certain Musa Kamaals who killed my buffaloes and witnessed the plunder of my goods for ten days by a creature of the governor Musa bin Salum, is detained too, as if to prevent evidence going to Zanzibar. I enclosed cheques for Rs 2,000 for men and goods and advised you of £400 which was to be sent by Mr Young to Fleming & Co for my use. I have had no medicine for years. A deserter who went with Hamees Wodim Tagh after losing my medicine box by handing it off to a countryman without orders, is probably with you now. His name is Baraka. My chronometers all dead. Please to thank Muhamad for his kindness and report it to the Sultan, with my salaam. Were he not so ugly by smallpox, I should like a photograph of him. I hope Kirk sent for vaccine virus. He says he would use it. I should like you to ask one of the American gentlemen at Zanzibar to forward a note which I enclose for my brother in Canada.

If anchored in a healthy spot and like London outcasts on Lord Shaftesbury's plan, taught to cook, wash, make and mend their clothes and all the jobs sailors can do, these African unfortunates might benefit the community, the teachers would be delivered from fear of blame by desertion, from administering proper discipline and if necessary afterwards trades learned at private workshops or when able, lessen the expenses of education by loading or unloading ships under proper inspection.

I would fain have written to you separately but you will excuse yours faithfully (I have no more paper here).

David Livingstone

If Mosquito curtains have come to hand, please to keep them for me, as I shall need them. I received two boxes in June/69 with wine and brandy, preserved meats and fruits, some Saturday Reviews and Punch but not a scrap of a letter!! These contained all the public news I have had since 1866.

61

Webb's Lualaba or Lacustrine
River.[89]
Across another great bend to
the west of about 100°.
March 25th, 1871

My Dear Kirk,

I very thankfully received your letter of 28th February,
1869 sent by Sheikh bin Nassib at Mamohela about 7 days
N.W. of Bambarre containing a welcome one from Agnes
to you. By it I first learned that you had taken unto yourself
a wife who has presented you with a daughter. Blessings on
them both. R.C. people think each has an angel – I only
know that the little ones are angels themselves and come as
ministering spirits of peace and love. I have but one regret
in looking back to my stationary missionary life and that is
that I did not play more with my children but I worked so
hard physically and mentally that in the evenings there was
seldom any fun left in me.

I thankfully accept your invitation to lodge with you at
Zanzibar but I feel so woefully far away and am going still
further in order to make a complete work of the exploration
of the sources of the Nile. I have been sorely let and hin-
dered in Manyema and reaction against the bloody Ujijian
slaving having set in I went off not without apprehension,
and until I get beyond the region of bloodshed I cannot feel
safe. It is not slave trade, it is slaking thirst for blood and
catching free people very many of whom die before reaching

the coast. I shall give you an episode which happened about a fortnight ago close by the spot where I write. My spirits are beyond measure depressed in writing on such matters for the public and I can only give half statements for fear of letting heartless dawdlers drawl from their club sofas 'exaggeration', 'overdrawing' etc. The restrained exposure of the vile Portuguese deeds on the Shire in my last book made me oblivious to everything else. My own and family interests were unheeded. Lord Palmerston sent a Queen's Counsel[90] to ask me 'what he could do to aid me as he was most anxious to serve me'. I could only think of the work in Africa and asked the East African ports to be opened to lawful commerce for all nations. It never occurred to me that he meant ought for myself or children till I was out here and Lord Palmerston dead.

The episode I mention was by Muhamad Bogharib's people, and he being the best man of all who have come to trade in Manyema you may, if you can, imagine the conduct of the people of the worst. Bin Hassani, Bin Mbegu and Bin Omar, the heads of the party sent to trade gave the Manyema near to Moene Lualaba 25 copper bracelets worth at Ujiji about $2\frac{1}{2}$ dollars – this was the trap – then went down the river and sold all the rest of their copper for ivory. Coming back they demanded ivory for the 25 rings and began to shoot the men in cold blood, and capture women and children and grass, cloth, goats and fowls. They continued their murdering for three days in a densely peopled district and carried off an immense number of women and children because Muhamad does not intend to trade here again. With all his goodness I have no doubt but he knew the plan and will receive his full share of the captives. They will come into Zanzibar as traders, and the people as *bought* slaves but there is not one slave among them, and to make the matter the more atrocious the very men who murdered and captured repeatedly declared to me that the people now victimised were remarkably civil and kind.

Thousands come over the river every market day to hold markets at various points for flour, cassava, beans, ground nuts, fish, salt, oil, bananas, plantains, sweet potatoes, sugar cane, grass, cloth, earthenware, iron ware as knives, spears, needles, fowls, sheep, goats, pigs, slaves, ivory etc, and it was particularly noticed that when the men of two districts were engaged in actual hostilities the women go from market to market with their wares unmolested. Women were never touched until now by these Muhamadans. As a rule not a slave is sold in Manyema except by the ruffian strangers. It would be only justice if the Sultan would set free all captives from Manyema as soon as they arrive. They were not traded for but murdered for. In talking with these Ujijians I always protest against shedding human blood. They think that rhyming over 'God is great', etc. all sin is forgiven. A slave of Thani bin Suelim of Ujiji named Yahood boasted in my hearing of having with his comrades killed one hundred people and burned 9 villages – all for a single string of red beads which a Manyema man tried in vain to steal. I said to him, 'You were sent to trade not to murder', he replied, 'We *are* sent to kill people, that is our work'. One of my people was killed, I suppose in blind revenge. A man was pinned to the ground with a spear near the 9 villages and I was sleeping in another close by. Three were killed at another village and we don't know who are friends and who have just cause to seek revenge of all strangers.

I find great difficulty in getting a canoe after the Bogharib feat of arms. All flee from us. Your men seem as eager for blood as others – all long to be able to brag of bloodshed.

That Sherif Bosher[91] has put me to great inconvenience by refusing to send me my own beads and other things while he stops to feast at my expense, he thinks that he and his three slaves are earning salary. I have sent orders to take the goods and give them to Msenyeghere, a trustworthy man. Awaha the other headman has enlarged scrotum (had it at Zanzibar and onwards, says now it pains him!! wants pay without work). I feel extremely thankful for all you did for me in the most trying circumstances a man could be placed in. I send a cheque for Rs. 4000 by Muhamad Bogharib.

Lualaba becomes smaller down here than stated in my despatch '2 to 4 miles', but it is still a mighty river from 1½ miles to 2 miles. Please to detain the despatch and letters if you hear of my being on the way down and near. I should like to rewrite all the hearsay written only in apprehension of never coming out.

Not a single line from Sir Paraffin Young since I left England and I have written him by every opportunity. The money I sent for was to be lifted from £1000 in Coutts' hands – mine not his. Letters may be in the box which Muhamad bin Saleh had my note to open and take out medicines and letters, but Mr Sherif refused to allow him. If you write to Seward[92] remember me kindly to him and to his wife. Take good care of your better half and child. Move about as often as you can, good people are scarce.

I am thankful to hear you say that my words have had some little effect at home. I have often said with a sore heart, I have laboured in vain and spent my strength for naught and in vain, but surely my work is with the Lord, and my judgement with my God. The cheering prospect of stopping the East Coast slave trade belongs to you, and therein I do greatly rejoice. The Sultan must get troops who will scour the mainland and catch the bloody thieves inland. By the counsel of an old man near him he is said to have parted with his Belooches[93] to save expense. He must not

Opposite : The Kebrabasa Gorge.
From a water-colour sketch by Kirk

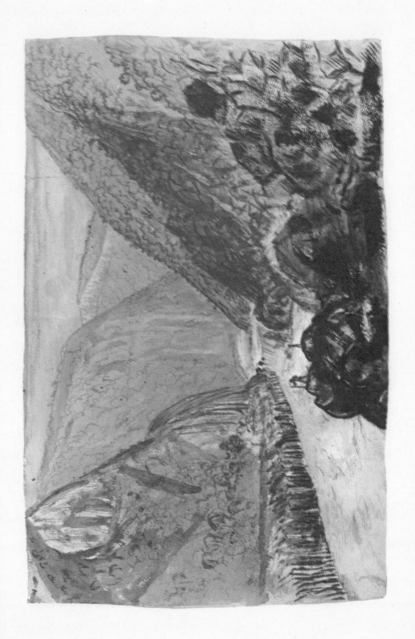

trust to Arabs. They are such liars. Their prophet lied to reform his countrymen, who now lie because it is ingrained in their constitutions.

In the event of detaining the despatch and letters, you might give the substance of my letter to you to the Government. I am rather anxious to give but little to the public. Four spurious publications were concocted from my letters on my journey across the continent. One, a five shilling book was sold in America and all over the world extensively as 'the book'. It was by a schoolmaster named Adams. Routledge sold a shilling book as mine at all the railways in England and America and offered me £20 to hold my peace about it. A secretary of the London Missionary Society issued a pamphlet *Dr Livingstone's life and travels* 'with a map by the author', and again advertised it with 'revised by himself'. Another secretary performed a like piece of villainy but palmed it off as from 'the Society', knowing that I would not injure a great institution doing work of priceless value in the world. Another secretary of the same Society indulged in a tirade, in a London Church, against me as 'morally guilty of the death of Mr Helmore'[94]. Cooley regularly proved me all wrong in the Athenaeum as soon as my letters reached home.

The Liambai which we found to be a mile broad was an 'undeveloped river' that ran under the Kalahari desert and was 'lost' and I was a fool to say that it was a river at all. Give Waller a hint not to answer him by name, it is the breath of life to him to be named. When I was silent he *entreated* me to argue the point of the Liambai with him, and Athenaeum shut out his letters when I only joked at him without naming him, 'the great apostle of hearsay geography'. Waller does not seem to know James Russell Lowell's poems. He is a Northerner and lashed the slaveocracy of the South when they uttered the same trash as the anthropologists till they were red hot with rage. 'The mass ought to labour and we lie on sofies' etc. etc.

A friend at Mamohela gave me a young soko or gorilla lately, she sits 18 inches high and is the most intelligent and least mischievous of all the monkeys I have seen. I could not take her with me as I am mobbed enough already, two sokos – she and I would not get a breath of air. She is to be kept for me at Ujiji. She walks on the backs of four fingers, the space between the first joint and second touching the ground, the nails and thumbs do not touch it. It is like the daft minister you knew, the legs are hitched forward as if the arms were crutches.

Musa Kamaals was detained many months and even sent back to Ujiji. He hid his letter as his wages depended on it. The 40 letters went off same day as Musa Kamaals. I suspect the Governor is guilty not to allow evidence of the plunder of my goods by his man Musa bin Salum going to the coast. Giving off my goods to his own creature who stopped the porters ten days while he plundered was villainy. The porters needed no one [?] they had come so far honestly and then Salum went off to buy ivory in Karangwe. I fear my two guns are abstracted from the box which Sherif nurses. You packed it and it is now repacked with I suspect Sherif's connivance, but I may be mistaken. It is suspicious that Sherif persisted in keeping it closed in spite of my written order to Muhamad bin Saleh to open it or send it entire. The men came without loads. A party went from us to Ujiji, told Sherif that I was near and waiting for him, invited him to come with them so he is inexcusable.

The Governor is very liberal with presents of foolscap paper, London maker's name Millington 1867, same as yours. Suspicious, I got a sheet of my own paper.

[David Livingstone]

62

May 14th, 1871[95]

Chakanja, Ludha's slave and Juma slave of Mamea, ringleaders of mutiny and the loudest in asserting that the
Consul told him not to go forward but to bring me back
and not to follow me if I went to a 'bad country', demanded
leave for 15 days to go and buy [?] of lambas where cheap
on our West and on my refusing went and told Abed what
ample rations they got at the coast and now would leave me.
I refused because Abed has got a canoe for me, price not
settled as the owner is sick, and I sent a party about six
miles off to examine another, see the owner, measure it and
come back with him if willing for the price next day. They
remained away six days. I could not trust these ringleaders
out of sight so sent other two of the slaves with guides to
order the first party back. These went on with them to kill
Manyemas and they did kill three men, and I [?] told them
I would never let them go anywhere unless I could go myself. A party is going to buy copper as it is smelted near us.
They killed a great number who stood in mute amazement
at the guns and their effects. These ringleading worthies in
everything that is bad hope to repeat this bloodshed because
they incur no danger and would get slaves. I never imagined
that human [?] or Muhammedan nature rather, could be
so atrociously vile. By the back [?] of this I give them a dismissal, twice refused to go North at Bambarre, then in the

way threw back their rations of beads, demanded double though what I gave was three times more than the Arabs give their slaves. I am glad to get rid of them by their own desire. They got two to follow them by loud talking of what they get at the coast and they know that my beads are nearly all at Ujiji. As to wages, you will know best. They compelled me to an advance, of six dollars at Bambarre a distinct breach with their engagement with you.

I am far West. Loeki or Lomame is at least 60° further – very broad – a true Lake Lincoln above. When on its west bank we shall be some six weeks only from the mouth of the Congo, the people swarming and friendly till abused by bloodhounds. They drink a cup of coffee after each meal, the trees are abundant. I am to get [?] some, it is well dried in the fruit rind.

If Waller likes to set a trap for Cooley, he might publish about my great Westing and draw the author of 'Inner Africa *laid* open' out on my stupidity in thinking Lualaba ought else but the Congo. Then publish this addendum. You will naturally, if very pigheaded like the great apostle of hearsay geography, swear I have been following the Congo instead of the Nile but here the mighty river takes a sweep to the East, takes in Lomame and becomes more grand than ever, 6 or 8 miles broad, with many very great inhabited islands in it before it joins or receives the *Kiziwa* which must be Lake Albert. Ivory is like grass, this is great news for Suahili and at 2 rings of copper a tusk.

I wish that licence were refused to all the Sultan's subjects for interior trade who are guilty of bloodshed causelessly.

David Livingstone

63

June 26th, 1871

On this page I intended to put an Arabic dismissal to the ringleaders. I use it now to say please do not be offended with palavers. I am really reduced to beggary notwithstanding all the bountiful provisions you with immense difficulty made for me and that too almost entirely by the villainy of the unmitigated drunken blackguard Sherif. His Banian owner [?] a British subject is in part to blame for he must have known his habits and his brandy when he imposed him on us. He is reported to have bought ivory with my goods and this ivory ought to be stopped at the custom house as is done in case of Arabs till he refunds. If Seyid bin Majid sends the list of goods left by Sherif you will judge of the extent of loss, if not then the case had better wait till I return. Remember that the list containing 12 Frasilahs sam-sam and the watch is that destroyed by Sherif. I have that of samsam 6 Frasilas, Langio 3 Do. and Pink 3 Do. All Dugumbe's[96] people saw the packet and think as he refused it to Dugumbe it is hidden, I feel sore most of all about the watch, though it is hard too to be living from hand to mouth in beggary, while my Banian slaves lived sixteen months in clover and idleness earning they supposed from five to seven dollars per month. They are independent of the Arabs but so they are of us and of honesty. I go West of this to Lomame – 60°, then buy a canoe if Dugumbe will advance the price and go south to the watershed and four fountains. Dugumbe is very friendly and a gentleman with more exploring enterprise in him than any other. He is going to sow and be here at Nyangwe for three years sending every now and then to Ujiji. Letters sent to him will be safe. His people will bring some goods for me from Ujiji and I shall share liberally with him. I might have mentioned that a dyke of basalt or other igneous rock cuts across the river 4 days of the canoe below this and the immense body of water is jammed rushing through the jutting ends which are not parallel and form whirlpools in which canoes wheel round and round helplessly. I am thankful I was not there for I would have been foremost in this and a cataract below it and no Makololo to help me.

I thought next of going up river to Kamolondo the broad part of Webb's Lake river but another cataract intervenes so I go due West on the 2nd day of New Moon about 9th July. In this jumble of odds and ends you will see how my mind is confused. I should have added up there that I don't go down river at present because in turning up Lomame from Lualaba I should probably meet the same basaltic dyke in the ascent for such dykes run a long way across country. Here I have a chance of cutting Lomame above it.

David Livingstone

I had to pay the carriers of Sherif's brandy. From first to last his own trade for ivory was what he followed shamelessly.

64

Unyanyembe
28th February, 1872

My Dear Kirk,

As I am sending by Mr Stanley for fifty freemen from Zanzibar to enable me to finish up my work I beg you to favour me with your influence with the Sultan that he may give me an able headman to lead them quickly here and continue with me till I have finished what I have still to do. A man of good character willing to work for me and on no account to attempt to inflict any private speculation on my expedition. – It is necessary to be particular on this point but if he proves himself a good energetic headman when we come into the country where ivory is abundant I shall try to make it worth his while to have come by means of my own good – if he has gone with a caravan previously he will know what duties he owes to the chief of it. We shall see on his arrival here by the manner in which he has obeyed Mr Stanley's instructions as to the donkeys and the men whether he is qualified to accompany me further. His duty as you very properly told others is to do what he is ordered and see that those under him do the same, without reference to the customs or practices of any other caravan.

I wish you to hand over to Mr Henry Stanley the sum of five hundred pounds (£500) out of the money placed in your hands for my use by H.M. Government to be laid out by him according to my arrangements with him and you will receive his receipt as a sufficient acknowledgement from me. He knows the kind of men and necessaries I need and I am sure your consular influence will be used to help him to get all I require and a speedy departure of the party inland. If you received two letters written hastily on 28th October 1871 and soon as I reached Ujiji one for you and the other for Lord Clarendon you may have been led to employ Banian or other slaves again instead of freemen. Do not hesitate please at once to discharge them no matter what expense may have been incurred – I have given Mr Stanley a draught on Bombay in case of your having spent all the money (£1000) sent by Government. No slaves must be sent for all those already employed came full of the idea that they were not to follow but force me back – and they positively swore (falsely of course) that you the consul had so instructed them. I enclose a receipt for a pocket chronometer from the captain of any man of war who may be able and willing to lend me one without interfering with the navigation of his own ship and before leaving this and pecuniary matters I would just add that haste is of vital importance and if any other way of getting money *quickly* suggests itself either from Mr Young or from my bankers Coutts & Co. please adopt it, and I hereby engage to refund the whole by cheque as soon as Mr Stanley's men reach Unyanyembe.

By some newspapers sent by Mr Webb to Mr Stanley I see that you are under the impression that goods and packets committed by you to Banians may reach Ujiji in about a month after delivery – the box packed by you was about *four* years in the . . . Goods and I suppose letters were sent by one Hassani and totally disappeared. Letters sent by Sherif were *fourteen* months in the way to Ujiji – one packet of them was destroyed. All the goods men sold off for

slaves and ivory but you were misled to cause Earl Gran-
ville to say in the House of Lords that all my wants had
been supplied. I need not enlarge further than give a bird's
eye view of your last supplies through Ludha and slaves –
the letters were fourteen months in the way to Ujiji and
came only through Mr Stanley accidentally seeing and seiz-
ing them for me. The slaves you sent would not accompany
him to Ujiji – why should they all have been taught *not* to
follow me. They told me that they lay four months at Baga-
moro – 3 bags of beads and one bale of cloth disappeared
the then two headmen ran riot on the goods here – one died
of smallpox and Athman the survivor broke the bolt and
keys of Mr Stanley's store in open day and stole his goods,
the journal then in his possession and a bale of calico he
had hidden but a case of brandy, which he said he knew
nothing about is not forthcoming. Dismissed.

I am &c
David Livingstone
H. M. Consul Inner Africa

My two silk mosquito curtains came from Captain White
and Bucklands curiosities of Natural History arrived from
Mr Murray. Please forward them. D.L.
Sherif and his slaves – Simon, Duce and Abahiru are all
at Unyanyembe enjoying the protection of Governor . . .
– the other Banian slave deserters are keeping out of the way
at Ujiji.

APPENDIX

∽∾∽

David Livingstone to Sir George Grey[97]

∽∾∽

H. M. Pioneer
Zambesi
November 15th, 1861

Dear Sir George,

We returned a few days ago from a three month's tour on the Lake Nyassa. A boat was carried past Murchison's cataracts, a distance of about forty miles. We then sailed sixty more before entering the Lake which is over 200 miles in length. It is from twenty to fifty or more miles broad and very deep. According to our present experience, a ship could only find anchorage near the shore but she might get a rock through her bottom a good way out besides. There are several rounded rocky islands, covered with dense forest, and uninhabited. Adjacent to these and also opposite all the rocky headlands detached rocks jut out or are covered with only a few feet of water. The Lake is surrounded by mountains or by high table lands, that appear as such; the eastern are higher than the western. A mountainous Cape which we named Cape Maclear, divides the southern end into two bays, one thirty, the other eighteen miles in length; the Lake has thus a forked appearance, and with the help of a little imagination, somewhat of the boot-shape of Italy. We went along the Western shore and found it a succession of bays, until, in the far north, the spurs of the mountains running sheer down to the water, scarcely afforded landing

places. In the South, while rounding Cape Maclear, no bottom was felt with our sounding line of 35 fathoms. In the
North, none was found with a fishing line of 696 feet, but
it broke in coming up and was therefore unsatisfactory. We
were there during the prevalence of the equinoctial gales and
found that tremendous seas, like those that play off Quillimane, rose in fifteen or twenty minutes.

An Arab dhow, lately built to carry slaves across, fled
from us twice to the Eastern shore. We could not cross,
though, at certain seasons, natives can in their canoes. We
never saw so many people anywhere else on its shores, and
slaving is the only trade: they were upon the whole very
civil. We were objects of great curiosity to them – no fines
were levied or dues demanded. Fish abound and the people
all seem fishermen, catching with large tremling nets – creels,
hooks, torches or poison. One species resembles salmon or
trout in shape, and goes up the rivers to spawn. It tastes
somewhat like herrings. Elephants and hippopotami very
tame. Alligators seldom kill men, so we could bathe in the
delicious cool waters when we liked. When we passed Lat.
11° 40′ South, we were in the borders of a tribe of Zulus
called Mazite or Mazatu, from the South (originally). They
live on the highlands, west of the north end of the Lake.
Very many skeletons and putrid bodies of the slain were
seen, and the land was depopulated. We heard, of course,
but one side of the story, and could form no opinion as to
the cause of this terrible slaughter. I met and had a short
interview with seven of these Mazite: they seemed as much
afraid of me as I ought to have been of them. We saw some
Mazite skulls on trees, and remains of burned bodies, so
they do not always come off unscathed. We returned about
as wise as we went, about the Rovuma; plenty of assertions
but in nothing did all agree, except that it is a very large
river.

Col. Rigby says in a letter, that most of the slaves entered at the port of Zanzibar came from Nyassa and a small steamer on it would break the neck of the traffic. Without knowing his opinion till lately, we have been working towards this end, and will now be employed the best part of the year carrying the steamer past the cataracts.

The Bishop will tell you all about his Mission better than I can. Three of his men came up the Shire in common country canoes, without knowing a word of the language or a bit of the way. This feat was never performed by white men before.

I am etc
David Livingstone

David Livingstone to Mrs Kirk

Murchison's Cataracts
December 17th, 1863

My Dear Mrs Kirk,

I offer my sincere thanks for your kind letter of condolence and am glad to think that ere this reaches you the long absent son will have returned once more to his home. He has been extremely useful in this Expedition and was always kind and obliging to every one. He was my right hand man and you may well be proud of such a son. I recommended him as strongly as I could to Earl Russell as an able and most trustworthy man and should he see any situation that would suit, if application were made for it through any member of Parliament I think he would be sure of it. Earl Russell would have no doubts as to his fitness, and this is the chief thing that stands in the way of applicants. I can sympathize with you cordially in your desire to see him again – I long sorely to see my children too, but patience is well tried in waiting for the rising of the river.

I question if he has lost much time. You perhaps know the saying that Doctors seldom are able to earn their bread until they have no teeth to eat it, but possibly you may wish to follow the good example of our Queen who gets all her children married as soon as they can look over the edge of the nest. I have written to him and enclosed all the letters (except a circular) that have come to hand.

Believe me with kind regards
Yours
David Livingstone

I dont recognize any letter from you among them.

Durris House
by Aberdeen
September 29th, 1874

My Dearest Mrs Webb,

Is not this too disgusting? Mr Waller has written to Mr Young telling him that there was a sale of Arrowsmith's effects and among them were all poor Papa's original maps. One of them was bought by Stamford, the map engraver, for a few shillings, if not pence and was the one which Arrowsmith altered to suit Cooley[98] and made Papa so bitter against him. Mr Young wrote to Mr Waller at once to secure it. I understood the other maps to be bought for the British Museum. Mr Waller says you can see where the alteration is made on the map. Is it any wonder that Papa spoke bitterly? We discovered some £2,000 of Papa's lying in Coutts' bank and Mr Young says that with all the sums coming in, there will be about £9,000 altogether. Mr Young has a document written by Papa at Lake Bangwalo about two months before his death which they think ought to be his will. In it he said he had given money for my brothers for their education and that all the rest should be divided between his daughters. Our Scotch Agent consulted our English Agent about it and the latter says that it will not legally hold good. I do not know how it will be settled but I would rather have it equally divided. I need not say that this is all *private* for you and Mr Webb alone. Anna Mary was to go to Kendal today. Mr Young is wild at Mr Dykes giving you all such a statement of our affairs because it was untrue. He says, if he had only been at home, he would have told Mr Dykes so and got Mr Waller to write the appeal simply as a testimonial without putting so many words in it and he is convinced we should have got £50,000.

Can you tell me if Mr Dykes gave his authority for his statement? I told Mr Young that I told Mr Waller it was the wording of the appeal that was wrong. In fact, I told him all about it as he wished to know, not having heard particulars. He says he wishes he had left Jerusalem a fortnight sooner. This is all private too, of course, and *no one* knows I tell you so much.

I hope Mr Webb's ankle is quite well. I have written to Mr Murray asking him why I have not received any more proofs. He has written to acknowledge that the printing of the work, the map and illustrations are all far advanced and no efforts of his will be wanting to get the book out in good time.

With much love to you all.

Believe me dearest Mrs Webb
Yours ever affectionately
Agnes Livingstone

NOTES
LIST OF LETTERS
INDEX

Z.D.— M

NOTES TO THE LETTERS

THE ZAMBESI EXPEDITION

1 Glasgow.
2 Foreign Secretary (1855–8).
3 Dr George Wilson, later Professor of Technology, University of Edinburgh.
4 Dr William Sharpey, Professor of Anatomy and Physiology, University College, London.
5 Assistant Director of Kew Gardens, younger son of Sir W. J. Hooker.
6 Admiralty hydrographer and an enthusiast for African exploration.
7 Sir William J. Hooker, Director of Kew Gardens.
8 J. H. Balfour, Professor of Botany, University of Edinburgh.
9 Major Tito Augusto Aracijo Secard.
10 S.S. *Pearl*, the vessel lent by the Colonial Office to convey the Zambesi Expedition to Tete.
11 This letter was handed to Kirk along with the preceding letter (No. 10) and its accompanying botanical and zoological instructions.
12 Dr Albert Roscher, who was sent to Africa by the King of Bavaria in 1858 and who arrived at Lake Nyasa two months after Livingstone.
13 A Portuguese official stationed at Tete; uncle of the British Vice-Consul at Quilimane.
14 Zulus settled to the south of the Zambesi, who exacted tribute from the Portuguese as well as the local natives.
15 Second in Command of the Zambesi Expedition, who resigned on June 30, 1858.

16   Surgeon and naturalist to the Niger Expedition, 1854.

17   Negro seamen from the coast of Liberia.

18   Portuguese commandant at Tete.

19   The stockade of Mariano.

20   Leading stoker, seconded from H.M.S. *Lynx* to the Zambesi Expedition.

21   Richard Frederick Burton, who explored in East Africa with J. H. Speke in 1857–9.

22   Medical Officer of *The Pioneer*.

23   A member of the Universities Mission to Central Africa which came to the Zambesi in 1861 with Bishop C. F. Mackenzie.

24   Lay superintendent of the U.M.C.A. party.

25   A Scottish Free Kirk minister who accompanied Mrs. Livingstone from the Cape to the Zambesi in 1862.

26   Livingstone's eldest son, who enlisted in the American army and died of wounds in a prisoner of war camp in 1864, aged eighteen.

27   Bishop Tozer, Mackenzie's successor, consecrated in Westminster Abbey on February 2, 1863.

28   Native porters brought by Livingstone from the Upper Zambesi.

29   One of the U.M.C.A. party.

30   The first page of this letter is missing.

31   Portuguese landowner of good family, said by James Stewart to have been banished from Portugal to East Africa for some offence.

32   Portuguese trader and slave-dealer at Mazaro.

33   Snr Manoel Gomez, brother-in-law of Bonga.

34   Portuguese Commandant at Quilimane.

35   Sir George Grey, K.C.B. (1812–98), High Commissioner and Governor of Cape Colony from 1854–61. He was relieved of his post in 1859 for encouraging the federation of South African states without Government approval but was reinstated in 1860. He warmly supported the Government Expedition to the Zambesi and was highly regarded by Livingstone.

36   Friend and companion of Tozer whom he succeeded as bishop in 1874.

37 Lord John Russell, Foreign Secretary 1859–65, created an earl in 1861.

38 James (later Sir) Young, founder of the paraffin works at Bathgate; a friend of Livingstone.

39 Bishop of Central Africa and leader of the U.M.C.A. party.

40 Commander of H.M.S. *Orestes*, a ship which gave Livingstone assistance during the Zambesi Expedition.

41 This note, written in the margin, was evidently added some time after the rest of the letter. Presumably, time would often elapse between writing a letter (or even between sections of a letter) and actually dispatching it to Kirk.

42 Native tribe inhabiting land to the west of the lower end of Lake Nyasa, otherwise known as the Anisa or Aisa.

43 A half-caste chief who rebelled against the Portuguese.

44 Livingstone's fifth child, born by the river Zouga in September 1852 and named after his friend William Oswell.

45 Bishop C. F. Mackenzie.

46 An honorary member of the Royal Geographical Society; published papers on African geography, 1841–74.

47 Prime Minister, 1859–65.

48 Livingstone's eldest son, Robert.

49 Dr William Sewell (1804–74), Warden of Radley College from 1852–62; ran into debt and went abroad to avoid his creditors.

50 A daughter of the banker Thomas Coutts.

51 Yao boys liberated from slavery by Livingstone.

NEWSTEAD ABBEY

52 Mrs. Webb, wife of W. F. Webb of Newstead Abbey.

53 Charles Livingstone, Moral Agent and General Assistant to the Zambesi Expedition.

54 Royal Geographical Society.

55 George William Fox, 9th Baron (1807–78), Privy Councillor (1840), Lord Lieutenant of Perth (1866); a keen geologist.

56 Livingstone's brother, Charles.

57 Cartographer and publisher, an original member of the R.G.S.

58 Secretary for India, created Viscount Halifax in 1866.

59   H.M. Consul at Zanzibar, 1858–61.
60   Livingstone's eldest daughter, born in 1847.
61   H.M. Consul at Johanna.
62   Sir Roderick Murchison, President of the R.G.S. and an eminent geologist.
63   Zanzibar landowner and former officer in the Indian navy who 'hired' native labour on his sugar plantations.
64   Friend and companion of Bishop Tozer.
65   German explorer and colonial pioneer in East Africa.
66   London Missionary Society Agent at Kuruman and father-in-law of Livingstone.
67   H.M. Consul and Political Agent at Zanzibar.
68   Governor-General of India, 1847–56.
69   Livingstone's London publisher.
70   Postmaster-General.
71   Permanent Under-Secretary at the Foreign Office, 1854–73.
72   See Letter 38.
73   The Church Missionary Society, founded in 1799 by evangelical churchmen.
74   First Bishop of Natal, deposed for heresy in 1863.
75   Livingstone was trained at the L.M.S. College at Ongar before going to Africa as an agent of the Society in 1840.
76   Owing to ill health, it was thought that the Consul would not return to Zanzibar.
77   This refers to the enclosed specimen of red powder.

INDIA
78   Two lines are missing from the third page of the letter.
79   Two lines are missing from the bottom of the page.
80   One word is illegible.
81   A word has been cut off at this point.

AFRICA
82   See Introduction; footnote on page 18.
83   Arab agent at Ujiji of the Hindu firm of Ludha Damji of Zanzibar.

84   A coarse cloth imported from America.

85   Sultan of Zanzibar, 1856–70.

86   A small section has been cut from the bottom of the second leaf of this letter, thus breaking into a paragraph on page 3 and removing the signature on page 4. Professor R. Coupland in *Livingstone's Last Journey* inserts the words 'so large, that I suspect I have been working on the sources of the Congo'; but it is unlikely that the letter was complete when Coupland referred to it, and this insertion is therefore assumed to be conjectural.

87   An Arab trader who came to Livingstone's aid in 1869 when he was dangerously ill near Ujiji.

88   Most of the boys were Africans rescued from slavery, who were being trained to earn their living as free men.

89   This letter is written on two sides of a proof sheet of an R.G.S. report dated November 8, 1869. After every available blank space had been covered closely Livingstone continued writing across the printed matter making it very difficult to decipher some of the words.

90   Mr A. Haywood, Q.C., an unofficial but regular political agent of Lord Palmerston.

91   An Arab trader who made free with Livingstone's stores at Ujiji.

92   H.M. Consul at Zanzibar, who succeeded Colonel Playfair.

93   Mercenary troops.

94   An agent of the London Missionary Society who went out to Linyanti in 1860 and died of malaria within a short time of his arrival.

95   This letter has no address and is written on a piece of blue foolscap paper bearing the word 'Quinine' and the initials 'J. K.'. This paper had been used to wrap the quinine which Kirk had sent up from the coast. On the other side is a letter addressed to Kirk, Letter 63. Both sides are written in the red native dye referred to by Livingstone in his diary (April 7, 1871). Many of the words in Letter 62 and Letter 63 are almost illegible, for over the years the red dye has faded and when the words are over cracks in the original folds of the wrapping paper they have all but disappeared. In his own copy of *Livingstone's*

Last Journals, Kirk wrote a note on page 129 saying that he had received a letter from Livingstone, dated June 26, 1871, showing that Livingstone had received quinine from him.

96   A wealthy and influential Arab trader.

APPENDIX

97   See note 35.

98   Livingstone refers to Cooley in Letter 61 as one who regularly proved him wrong.

LIST OF LETTERS

The Zambesi Expedition

(1) Hamilton, January 4th, 1858
(2) 12 Kensington Palace Gardens, January 14th, 1858
(3) 12 Kensington Palace Gardens, January 21st, 1858
(4) 15 Whitehall Place, January 22nd, 1858
(5) 50 Albemarle St., January 26th, 1858
(6) Manchester, January 28th, 1858
(7) 18 Hart Street, February 17th, 1858
(8) London, February 22nd, 1858
(9) Glasgow, February 28th, 1858
(10) S.S. *Pearl* (at sea off Madeira), March 18th, 1858
(11) S.S. *Pearl*, April 15th, 1858
(12) Off Shupanga, July 21st, 1858
(13) Island of Pita, August 25th, 1858
(14) Dakana Moiro Island, October 17th, 1859
(15) Shamoara, October 29th, 1859
(16) [?], November 3rd, 1859
(17) Shupanga, November 6th, 1859
(18) Murchison Cataracts, June 2nd, 1863
(19) Cataracts of Shire, July 5th, 1863
(20) [?], ?1863
(21) Malango, August 8th, 1863

(22) Murchison's Cataracts, December 9th, 1863
(23) Tavistock Hotel, Covent Garden, July 28th, 1864
(24) Hamilton, September 1st, 1864

Newstead Abbey

(25) Newstead Abbey, October 17th, 1864
(26) Newstead Abbey, October 21st, 1864
(27) Newstead Abbey, November 3rd, 1864
(28) Newstead Abbey, November 7th, 1864
(29) Newstead Abbey, November 24th, 1864
(30) Newstead Abbey, November 25th, 1864
(31) Newstead Abbey, November 27th, 1864
(32) Newstead Abbey, December 1st, 1864
(33) Newstead Abbey, December 8th, 1864
(34) Newstead Abbey, December 12th, 1864
(35) Newstead Abbey, December 19th, 1864
(36) Newstead Abbey, February 11th, 1865
(37) Newstead Abbey, February 13th, 1865
(38) Newstead Abbey, February 14th, 1865
(39) Newstead Abbey, February 24th, 1865
(40) Newstead Abbey, February 28th, 1865
(41) Newstead Abbey, March 5th, 1865
(42) Newstead Abbey, March 21st, 1865
(43) Newstead Abbey, March 24th, 1865
(44) Newstead Abbey, March 27th, 1865
(45) Newstead Abbey, March 28th, 1865
(46) Newstead Abbey, April 5th, 1865
(47) Newstead Abbey, April 14th, 1865
(48) Newstead Abbey, April 30th, 1865

(49) 8 Dover St., London, May 13th, 1865
(50) Burnbank Road, Hamilton, June 8th, 1865
(51) Burnbank Road, Hamilton, June 24th, 1865
(52) Newstead Abbey, July 30th, 1865

India
(53) Poonah, September 20th, 1865
(54) Bombay, November 15th, 1865
(55) Bombay, December 2nd, 1865
(56) Bombay, December 13th, 1865
(57) Bombay, January 1st, 1866

Africa
(58) Msama's country, September 12th, 1867
(59) Ujiji, May 30th, 1869
(60) Bambarre, Manyema country, November 2nd, 1870
(61) Webb's Lualaba, March 25th, 1871
(62) [?], May 14th, 1871
(63) Nyangwe, June 26th, 1871
(64) Unyanyembe, February 28th, 1872

Appendix
1. David Livingstone to Sir George Grey, November 15th, 1861
2. David Livingstone to Mrs Kirk, December 17th, 1863
3. Agnes Livingstone to Mrs Webb, September 29th, 1874

INDEX

Names enclosed in brackets indicate alternative spellings.